Current Research in Egyptology III

December 2001

Edited by

Rachel Ives
Daniel Lines
Christopher Naunton
Nina Wahlberg

BAR International Series 1192
2003

Published in 2016 by
BAR Publishing, Oxford

BAR International Series 1192

Current Research in Egyptology III

ISBN 978 1 84171 558 2

BAR Publishing is the trading name of British Archaeological Reports (Oxford) Ltd.
British Archaeological Reports was first incorporated in 1974 to publish the BAR
Series, International and British. In 1992 Hadrian Books Ltd became part of the BAR
group. This volume was originally published by Archaeopress in conjunction with
British Archaeological Reports (Oxford) Ltd / Hadrian Books Ltd, the Series principal
publisher, in 2003. This present volume is published by BAR Publishing, 2016.

Printed in England

BAR
PUBLISHING

BAR titles are available from:

BAR Publishing
122 Banbury Rd, Oxford, OX2 7BP, UK
EMAIL   info@barpublishing.com
PHONE   +44 (0)1865 310431
FAX   +44 (0)1865 316916
www.barpublishing.com

CONTENTS

FOREWORD

Following a successful inaugural event at the University of Oxford and an expanded second at the University of Liverpool, the *Third Symposium for Current Research in Egyptology* was held in December 2001, at the University of Birmingham. The symposium, based on the model set up by Christina Riggs and Angela McDonald at Oxford, was again successful in bringing together UK-based graduate students of Egyptology to provide an opportunity to disseminate the results of their research. It also served to encourage communication between an otherwise disparate group of students spread across the various Egyptological institutions throughout the country. Indeed, speakers came from nine different institutions and the papers presented illustrated well the broad range of topics currently being studied throughout the United Kingdom. Dr Anthony Leahy introduced the symposium, the scope of which was widened somewhat this time by the inclusion of some speakers not formally attached to a university, and also of Dr Aidan Dodson, who kindly stepped in to fill an unexpected gap in the programme.

We would like to thank the Department of Archaeology and Ancient History and School of Historical Studies at the University of Birmingham, and especially Dr Anthony Leahy, Dr Lisa Montagno Leahy, Sue Bowen and Bob Arnott for help and support in organising the conference. Our thanks also to Sally Mallard and the Birmingham University Graduate School for their sponsorship, and to Ashley Cooke and Fiona Simpson for their advice. For help during the conference we are grateful to Roberto Gozzoli, Philip Kay and Julie McEwen. Finally, we would like to thank David Davison for continued support of the symposium.

At the time of writing, the CRE symposium has enjoyed a very successful fourth event, hosted by the Institute of Archaeology, University College London. The fifth symposium is due to be held in Durham in 2004.

Rachel Ives
Daniel Lines
Christopher Naunton
Nina Wahlberg
May 2003

SYMPOSIUM PAPERS NOT PUBLISHED IN THIS VOLUME (in alphabetical order)

The Origins of the Cattle Cult in Ancient Egypt
Michael Brass
Cape Town University

The Mummy's Body as an Object of Horror
Rachael Dann
The University of Durham

Duke Alexander's Sarcophagi
Dr Aidan Dodson
Bristol University
Published as 'Duke Alexander's Sarcophagi', *Archiv Orientální* 70 (2001), 329-36.

Ritual and Initiation at Abydos: A Context for Narrative Biography in the Nineteenth Dynasty
Elizabeth Frood
Queen's College, Oxford

Writing a History of Ancient Egypt: Some Theoretical Issues
Roberto Gozzoli
The University of Birmingham

Amenhotep III, his Blue Crowns, and their Progeny
Tom Hardwick
Queen's College, Oxford

The Range of Meaning in Middle Egyptian 'Second Tenses'
Marko Hyypia
University College, Oxford

Foreigners in Egypt During the New Kingdom
Amir Kamal
The University of Liverpool

A Curious Middle Kingdom Stela from Birmingham
Daniel Lines
The University of Birmingham
Published as 'A Curious Middle Kingdom Stela in Birmingham', *JEA* 87 (2001), 43-54.

Ptolemaic Cities in Space – A Case Study of Fayumic Settlements
Katja Mueller
Peterhouse College, Cambridge

Professor Plumley, Qasr Ibrim and the EES in Nubia
Christopher Naunton
The University of Birmingham / EES

The Bone, Ivory and Wooden Labels of the Late Predynastic and Early Dynastic: The Iconography of Kingship
Kathryn Piquette
The Institute of Archaeology, University College London

The Lotus Reborn: The Creation and Distribution of the *Description de l'Égypte*

Andrew Bednarski

The Napoleonic *Description de l'Égypte* is a unique work in the study of discipline formation. The corpus was the result of research done during the strategically odd and ill-fated French military invasion of Egypt between 1798 and 1801. In 1802, with the return of the Savants who had completed the research, steps were taken by the French government to publish the accumulated data. Yet despite nearly constant efforts to publish the material, the work did not see completion until 1828. Remarkably, this state project persevered throughout the twenty-six year span, a period that witnessed the fall of Napoleon's government, his return, and the eventual re-establishment of the French monarchy. The goal of the corpus was ambitious: nothing short of the description of Egypt's antiquities, contemporary state and natural history. The work took the form of nine in-folio volumes of text, ten folio volumes of images that used 837 copper engravings, and an atlas. Examples of the *Description*'s images can be seen in the following: Figure 1, which reproduces the work's imperialistic frontispiece;[1] Figure 2, which depicts an image from the northernmost limit of the French campaign, Alexandria; and Figure 3, which depicts the temple of Philae, the southernmost limit of the army's expedition. Once completed, the data contained in the work represented the first large-scale, systematic study of Egypt. It is due to both the work's goal and its execution that many histories of Egyptology mention the *Description de l'Égypte* as the first seminal point in the development of the subject. Despite such statements, however, explorations of this notion are rare in the English language. My current research is an attempt to move away from the iconic status that the work has developed in English literature in order to explore better its historical importance. This article will attempt to do this by first examining the intellectual roots of the *Description* and then exploring the work's dissemination and usage by the French government.

Roots

The history of European interest in Egypt and the build-up to the Napoleonic invasion are well documented in numerous sources.[2] As a result, I do not intend to produce a chronological account of Western attention towards, and works upon, Egypt. Nor do I intend to analyse the late eighteenth century European intellectual climate and the impact that it had on the development of the work. Instead, I would like briefly to explore the influence of prior works on the *Description de l'Égypte*. When examining these earlier works, I would also like to address the issue of how prepared the French Savants were to conduct research in Egypt.

It is possible to view the Napoleonic corpus as one work within a literary continuum. By envisioning such a continuum, it is also possible to isolate texts that were influential on the *Description*'s development. Prior to the Napoleonic work, 'descriptions' of countries outside Europe were not unheard of. A good example of such a work is Olfert Dapper's *Description de l'Afrique*, published in Flemish in 1670, republished in English in the same year and eventually translated into French in 1686. Dapper's *Description* covered a wide variety of topics on African countries and its second chapter is dedicated to Egypt.

A second and particularly influential work on the Napoleonic *Description* can be found in the writings of Benoit de Maillet. Letters by de Maillet, written during his time as *Ancien Consul de France* in Cairo, were published in 1735 by Jean Baptiste le Mascrier under the title *Description de l'Égypte*. Aside from the title, this work shares a similar ideological perspective to that of the Napoleonic *Description*. Le Mascrier mentioned Egypt's long history and stated that it was perhaps the country most ignored at the time of his writing.[3] He emphasised Egypt's importance to Europe by stressing historical, classical links between the two regions.[4] Le Mascrier encouraged further investigations of Egypt, stating that the Arts and Sciences should be returned to the Egyptians, a people who were once the most celebrated in the universe.[5] Finally, he lamented the state of Egyptian scholarship, claiming that investigations tended not to

---

[1] For further information on the frontispiece's imperial nature and propaganda value, see Piussi 1999.

[2] For example: Clément 1960; Laissus 1973; Laurens 1987; Beacour et al. 1989; Laurens 1990; Kalfatovic 1992; Bret 1999.

[3] le Mascrier 1735, iii.

[4] ibid. iii.

[5] ibid. iv.

go far enough into relevant subjects,[6] and even naming the French *République des Lettres* as being lax with regard to Egyptian research.[7]

Similarly, the Napoleonic *Description*'s *Historical Preface* emphasised Egypt's long history[8] and supposedly strong association with, and influence upon, Greece and Rome.[9] Napoleon's *Description* echoed le Mascrier's claims that more in-depth work was needed on Egypt, claiming that, until its development, many eras of history had been ignored.[10] Finally, the very first page of the *Preface* mentions Egypt as being the birthplace of the Arts and Sciences, a theme that recurs throughout the work, and that the goal of the French Savants was to return these Muses to the land of their origin.

By the early 1700s, travel to Egypt multiplied as a result of a large diffusion of publications.[11] One such important publication was Captain Frederik Ludvig Norden's *Travels in Egypt and Nubia*, published in London in 1741 and then in Copenhagen in 1755 before being published in Paris. Like the Napoleonic corpus, Norden's work emphasised a visual account of Egypt and the engraved plates that it provides are extremely important to understanding those of the *Description*.[12] While some authors have argued that the first truly accurate images of Egypt came with the Napoleonic *Description*, such assertions have been challenged. Marie-Louise Buhl, for example, stated that the importance of Norden's work lies in the fact that sixty years before the French expedition, he made '...excellent maps of the Nile valley as well as precise descriptions and representations of as many monuments and landscapes he was able to'.[13] Yet similarities between the *Description* and Norden's *Travels* are also evident in their texts. Like the *Description*, Norden's work endorsed the notion that the ancient Egyptians had particularly influenced other cultures, but had long since fallen from grace. This view is made explicit in Norden's address to the King of Denmark: 'In reading the following account of a country, that was once the model to other nations, but is now sunk through tyranny into the greatest ignorance and brutality...'.[14] This statement is strongly echoed in the following passage from the *Description*'s *Historical Preface*: '*Cette contrée, qui a transmis*

ses connoissance à tant de nations, est aujourd'hui plongée dans la barbarie'.[15]

A second work of the same period is Pococke's *A Description of the East and some other Countries*, published in London in 1743 and followed by numerous re-editions and translations. Like Norden, Pococke wanted to provide a visual record of Egypt's monuments and gave the reader numerous maps and plans. Yet the work also paralleled the interests of earlier writers and those of Napoleon's Savants in its subject matter. Although originally intending to provide the plans of Egyptian buildings and discuss the orders of Egyptian architecture, Pococke was eventually persuaded to deliver '...as short and perfect an account as he could of Egypt, and to add something of the government, customs, and natural history, as the latter would also give a general idea of the Turkish polity and manners'.[16]

In 1772 Niebuhr published his *Beschreibung von Arabien*, a supposedly broad encyclopaedia based on his expedition's findings. A French version appeared a few years later, and a popular version of the work, translated by Robert Heron, was published in Edinburgh in 1792.[17] In Niebuhr's work, the notion of Egypt's historical pre-eminence[18] and the notion of the country having lost its glory is once again evident.[19] Also, Niebuhr attributed Egypt's decline and poverty to its contemporary government[20] a notion clearly picked up by the Napoleonic Savants and evident in the *Historical Preface*.[21]

Two other works that had a great influence on Napoleon's *Description* were Savary's *Letters on Egypt*, published between 1785-6 and Constantin-François Chasseboeuf, *Comte de Volney*'s, *Voyage en Égypte et en Syrie*, published in 1787. Both works continue the notion of Egypt as a particularly formative power on Europe.[22] In chapter nineteen of Volney's work, the author also expressed dissatisfaction with the current state of knowledge regarding the Great Pyramids and urged further research.[23] In this chapter Volney also mentioned how beneficial it would be for another power to control Egypt: preferably a '*Nation amie des beaux-arts*', who might further unlock its ancient

6 ibid. v.

7 ibid. vi.

8 Fourier 1809, i.

9 ibid. i.

10 ibid. ix.

11 Leclant 1999, 125.

12 Pinault-Sørensen 1999, 160.

13 Buhl et al. 1986, 37.

14 Norden 1757.

15 Fourier 1809, ii.

16 Pococke 1743, iii.

17 Bidwell 1994, vi.

18 Heron 1792, 149.

19 ibid. 51.

20 ibid. 52.

21 Fourier 1809, iv.

22 Savary 1787, vol. I, viii and Volney 1787, vi.

23 Volney 1787, 244.

secrets.[24] The Napoleonic *Description* expands on the idea of a country controlling Egypt. In fact, it speaks of foreign control of Egypt as if it were a foregone conclusion, with the *Historical Preface* claiming that there had not been, in the West or in Asia, one considerable power that did not set its sights on Egypt nor failed to view it, in some fashion, as a natural appendage.[25] Leclant felt Savary and Volney's works were particularly special resources for the Savants who compiled the *Description*. He described them as documentary works, far from the 'Egyptian mirage' that many learned Western travellers presented. He also claimed that both works supplied the Napoleonic expedition to Egypt and the *Description* with abundant, authentic information.[26]

Aside from the above-mentioned works, which covered many topics eventually discussed in the Napoleonic *Description*, the French Savants had different resources to which they might turn. A strong history of less academic, travellers' accounts predates Napoleon's *Description*. Also, as alluded to in the previous paragraphs, Classical sources spoke of the Orient. Finally, it must be remembered that European scholars also knew of a biblical Orient.

Yet with all of these works in existence, the question must be asked: how prepared were the French Savants for their exploits in Egypt? This question is a thorny one. Numerous sources state that the Savants had access to a library while in Egypt.[27] The idea of a Savant library has even been expanded into the following popular view: 'The intellectual contingent brought along a large library, containing practically every book on the land of the Nile available in France'.[28] Given that the military campaign was organised with extreme secrecy, for fear of early British intervention, and that the final destination was not revealed to the majority of the participants until after the expedition left France, I find the latter statement unlikely. Purchasing large numbers of books on Egypt seems like a poor way for the French government to have concealed its ultimate goal and I have yet to find any evidence to support the rampant collection of such works. On the issue of the Savants' academic preparedness when confronting Egypt, it seems reasonable to assume that various expedition members were familiar with Classical, biblical and contemporary sources relating to Egypt. Nor does it

seem impossible that certain works devoted to Egypt existed in the Savant's library. Yet despite these facts, it would appear that the vast majority of sources dealing with Egypt would only have been available for comparison with the collected data after the Savants' return to France. This line of thinking is in keeping with the notion that the Savants were not chosen in order to produce the *Description*, a decision that developed much later in the expedition, but rather to build a modern infrastructure, as stated by Dewachter and Gillispie[29] and Dhombres.[30]

Branching out

A rather large chronological leap forward will bring us from the compilation and sorting of data by the Savants, begun in 1802, to the eventual distribution of the *Description*, begun in 1810. When investigating the dissemination of the corpus, numerous sources are available for examination. The most notable is a large register in the *Bibliothèque Nationale*, entitled *Commission d'Égypte 20, Vente et Distribution*, and given the acquisition number NAF 21953. This 402 page volume records sales information for the *Description* between 1810 and 1860 and it would appear possible to compile its information into a lengthy distribution list. The register also contains a long list of subscribers to the second edition *Description* and this list can also be found within the second edition itself. Another such list of subscribers can be found at the beginning of Louis Reybaud's *Histoire scientifique et militaire de l'expédition française en Égypte*.[31] Finally, distribution information can be found in an eleven volume series of registers devoted to the overall development of the Napoleonic *Description* between 1802 and 1827. This series, entitled *Délibérations de la Commission chargée de diriger l'exécution de l'ouvrage sur l'Égypte*, has the following acquisition numbers in the *Bibliothèque Nationale*: MF 15281-15287, NAF 3584, MF 15288, NAF 3586, NAF 3587. It is not my goal to assemble all of these and possibly other distribution sources into one, large, comprehensive list. Instead, for the sake of analysis, I have contented myself with a sample population. More specifically, I will discuss the *Description*'s dissemination by using a distribution list that I created with the eleven volume series of registers.

This distribution list has 427 workable entries. Using the titles given for each person or place mentioned in an entry, it is possible to divide the list into ten broad categories. These categories, and the number of entries that they contain, can be seen in Table 1.

---

[24] ibid. 256.
[25] Fourier 1809, i.
[26] Leclant 1999, 127.
[27] See Bourienne 1830, 207-8; Guémard 1928, 149; Dewachter and Gillispie 1987, 6; Dhombres and Dhombres 1989, 97.
[28] Ceram 1954, 50.

[29] Dewachter and Gillispie 1987, 2.
[30] Dhombres and Dhombres 1989, 104.
[31] Reybaud 1830, 36.

When creating Table 1, I decided that a category would only be established if more than three entries could be placed within it. The one exception to this rule is the category of booksellers and traders, due to the importance of the entries listed.

The first category contains a variety of titles: barons, dukes, prefects, lieutenant generals and even kings. Essentially, however, it is possible to view this category as representing people of relatively high social standing both inside and outside France. Creating a category with such a mixture of people and titles seemed appropriate, as the social spheres from which many of these titles came overlapped. For example, one entry dated 27 March 1821 refers to a copy ordered for 'Baron Almera, *Lieutenant Général*'.[32] As a result, it did not seem appropriate to classify Almera solely as a baron or a lieutenant general. A system of classification of this sort enables one to see broad trends in the *Description*'s distribution without being overly confined by the variety of titles presented in the eleven volume register. For example, the title prefect occurs several times in the category of government official, yet also appears in the first category. The difference between the categories, however, is that the prefects listed in the first category have additional noble or military titles.

The second, third and fourth categories are self-explanatory. Category five is interesting, as every member listed therein was also a contributor to the *Description*.[33] The following category contains people whose only title is that of member of the *Commission des Sciences et Arts*, the governmental commission that undertook the creation of the *Description*. It should be noted, however, that other commission members can be found within other categories. The category of booksellers/traders is not as well represented in the eleven volume series of registers as it is in other distribution lists. In fact, only two booksellers are listed: Debure, *père et fils, libraires de la Bibliothèque Impériale* and Tilliard *frères, libraires*. Incidentally, these two booksellers were originally given the exclusive right to sell the *Description* inside and outside France.[34] Finally, there is the category that I have labelled miscellaneous. This section contains a wide range of titles and occupations, but no pattern has been observed amongst them.

What does this distribution list reveal? Due to the scholastic nature of the *Description*, it might be assumed that the largest group seeking to purchase or receive it might have been individual academics, academic institutions or learned societies. The most obvious thing that the sample population reveals, however, is that the eleven volume series of registers recorded the largest concentration of copies going to civic and military leaders inside France and beyond its borders. The *Description* was given, as a gift, to important people and/or heads of state and this fact might have increased the numbers in the first category of Table 1. Another factor that might have contributed to the dominance of the first category is the work's initial cost. The first edition was printed in four different qualities and one volume could cost as much as 6000 Francs.[35] By the 1830s, however, the price of the work had fallen dramatically. By this period, it was possible to purchase the first section for the following amounts: 750 Francs for a volume with one coloured plate; 800 Francs for sixteen coloured plates; 1,200 Francs for a vellum edition; and 1,350 Francs for a vellum edition of the earliest impressions of plates, retouched by hand.[36] In short, such prices might have made the work less attractive, or less accessible, to other groups listed in Table 1.

As a point of interest, I feel it pertinent to mention the second edition of the *Description*, produced between 1821 and 1829 by C. L. F. Panckoucke. This printing took the form of twenty-six volumes of text and twelve volumes of plates. The cost for the volumes of text was either six or eight Francs and the cost of the volumes of plates was ten Francs.[37] This edition was considerably less expensive than the first and, as a result, may have been more widely distributed to other specific groups. In any case, this edition has little consequence on the sample population, which was primarily concerned with the distribution of the first edition.

A less obvious fact that can be deduced from Table 1 actually relates to academic groups. I have made the distinction between entries that refer to specific institutions and entries that refer to cities/towns. In reality, however, this distinction is artificial, as many copies allocated to cities/towns would likely have ended up in academic institutions in those locales. With this in mind, the two categories might be combined, thereby bringing the total to 106. Such an addition makes academic institutions the second largest group represented in the eleven volume register and is more in keeping with the original expectation of scholarly interest in the *Description*.

---

[32] MF 15287, 5.
[33] As evident from a list of contributors dated 8 January 1810, MF 15288, 100.
[34] MF 15282, 12 May 1809, 183.

[35] Brunet 1834, 425.
[36] Baring 1838, 19.
[37] ibid. 20.

Also, it should be noted that all of the cities and towns listed in Table 1 are French. As a result, the eleven volume register apparently represents an emphasis on the work being specifically distributed to civic centres within France.

This distribution list can also give insight into the copies of the work that were sent outside France. Thus far I have been able to identify the foreign copies represented in Table 2.

Table 2 shows the priority that the French government placed on copies sent abroad. Out of the twenty-eight entries listed six are dedicated to foreign princes, kings or emperors; two mention foreign military leaders; three refer to foreign government officials; three mention French officials abroad; eight refer to French legations or ambassadors; two mention institutions; and the remaining four refer to various individuals. To summarise, Table 2 illustrates that the majority of copies were sent abroad to heads of state, important members within foreign governments or French political representatives. It should be noted that this fact is in keeping with the general trend observed in Table 1.

The harvest

After reviewing the above information, one question must be asked: why did the French government send the great work to such highly placed people outside France? Several factors appear to have motivated such action. Aside from the work being given as what appears to be an honest gift, nationalism seems to have been one such factor. This very impetus is evident in the eleven volume series and takes the form of a letter from the government commission in charge of creating the work to the Minister of the Interior who oversaw the project. This letter is dated 11 December 1820 and was written by the Commissioner. The letter concerns a decision to postpone the delivery of a copy of the work to the French legation in Prussia. The author of this letter states that he thought the point of distributing the work to a legation was to add to the impact of the embassy by giving it a monument that demonstrates to the outside world the degree to which the Arts and Sciences were cultivated and honoured within the French kingdom. He goes on to say that he thought the copies that were addressed to London, Vienna and St. Petersburg had the same objective.[38] From this passage and the above evidence, it becomes apparent that the *Description* was partially meant to demonstrate to the outside world the grandeur of France.

Additionally, it appears that the work was meant to be introduced to countries in a manner that was deemed to have significant impact: i.e. by means of the French embassies or by being directed to heads of state or prominent institutions.

Another example of the French government's strategic distribution of the work can be seen in a copy eventually sent to Egypt. On 2 January 1821, a Minister wrote a letter requesting one copy of the *Description*'s geographic map be sent to the officer attached to the Viceroy of Egypt.[39] This order is further discussed in a following passage of the same date. In it, it is suggested that one copy of the map be printed and given to Mr. Osman, a French official. This letter stresses, however, that the work was solely intended for use by Mr. Osman and his officers. Finally, the letter states that, as the French King had made a gift of several copies of the *Description* to various rulers, such a token might be a timely gift to the Pasha, who was avidly researching works of the same genre, and one that Mr. Osman might be able to deliver.

On 13 January 1821, this issue was again addressed.[40] This entry stated that the Foreign Affairs Minister requested that a copy of the work be placed at the Pasha's disposal. As a result plans were made for one copy, printed on fine paper, to be given to the Baron Pasquier, the Secretary Minister of State and Foreign Affairs and the officer attached to the Viceroy of Egypt. Three days later, a final letter was written, confirming the plan.[41]

Conclusion

While the *Description* may have come to symbolize a new science, that of Egyptology, and used new, quantitative methods in its research, it was well rooted in academic traditions. Despite this fact, it appears that many relevant works would only have been accessible upon the Savants' return to France, thereby forcing them to be largely self-sufficient in their explorations of Egypt. This notion makes the work that they accomplished appear all the more impressive, particularly when one considers the military hardships under which the Savants toiled. The reader of the *Description* quickly realizes that it was never intended to be a purely academic work. Similarly, this notion is evident in the corpus' dissemination. By examining its distribution an interesting insight into the groups of people who

---

[38] MF 15286, 174.

[39] ibid. 175.
[40] MF 15286, 176.
[41] ibid. 176.

requested copies of the work and, more importantly, those groups/people deemed worthy enough to receive copies is gained. As a result, it appears that, alongside its scholastic importance, the work became a tangible, symbolic, exportable representation of French culture.

Acknowledgements
Special thanks to the Thomas Mulvey Fund for assisting in my research.

Andrew Bednarski
Gonville and Caius College
University of Cambridge

Table 1: Distribution Categories

Category	Number of Entries
Royalty, Nobility and Military Leaders	135
Cities and Towns	59
Institutions	47
Government Officials	39
Engineering Corps Members and Engineers	22
Commission Members	16
Ambassadors, Legations and Embassies	7
Printers	6
Booksellers and Traders	2
Miscellaneous	87
Uncertain entries	2
Total	429

Table 2: Foreign Distribution

	Person to whom a copy was allocated	Type of copy	Number ordered	Year ordered
Austria				
1.	*Empereur d'Autriche* (Emperor of Austria)	1st print	1	1815
1a.	Young, *bibliothécaire de S.M. l'Empereur d'Austriche* (librarian for H. M. the Emperor of Austria)	vellum	1	1815
2.	Frimont, *baron, commandant supérieur des troupes Autrichiennes* (Baron, Upper Commander of Austrian troops)	2nd print	1	1816
3.	*Palais de légation française de légation de Vienne* (Palace of the French legation of the legation to Vienna)	fine	1	1820
4.	Prince de Metternich, *ministre des affaires étrangères de S.M. l'Empereur d'Autriche* (Minister of Foreign Affairs to H. M. the Emperor of Austria)	vellum	1	1819
Britain				
5.	Castléragh, lord	vellum	1	1819
6.	*Palais de légation française de légation de Londres* (Palace of the French legation of the legation to London)	vellum	1	1820
7.	*Muséum britannique* (British Museum)	?	1	1824
8.	Wellington, *duc* (Duke)	1st print	1	1816
8a.	Wellington, lord	?	2	1819
Denmark				
9.	de Kaan, *ministre de l'intérieur au Danemark* (Minister of the Interior of Denmark)	fine	1	1819
10.	*Roi de Danemark* (King of Denmark)	vellum	1	1819
Egypt				
11.	Pasquier, *baron, ministre secrétaire d'état des affaires étrangères, officier attaché au Vice Roi d'Égypte* (Baron, Secretary Minister of State of Foreign Affairs, officer attached to the Viceroy of Egypt)	fine	1	1821
Greece				
12.	Pouqueville, *ancien consul de France à Patras* (Ancient Consul of France to Patrai)	fine	1	1822
Italy				
13.	*Bibliothèque de l'école française à Rome* (Library of the French School in Rome)	?	1	1819
14.	*Comte de Cicognara, président de l'académie de Venise, correspondant de l'Institut de France* (Count...President of the Academy of Venice, correspondant of the Institut of France)	fine	1	1819
15.	Grenier, *comte* (Count)	1st s	1	1815
16.	Karcha, *chevalier, chargé d'affaires de Toscane* (Knight, charged with the affairs of Tuscany)	fine	1	1821
17.	*Palais de légation française de légation de Rome* (Palace of the French legation of the legation to Rome)	fine	1	1820
17a.	A copy was sent to the Duke of Blacas, and was to be shared between the Ambassador and the legation's library	fine	1	1826

Ottoman Empire				
18.	*Ambassadeur de France en Turquie* (Ambassador of France in Turkey)	?	1?	1821
19.	*Légation française à Constantinople* (French legation in Constantinople)	fine	1	1821
Prussia				
20.	*Palais de légation française de légation de Berlin* (Palace of the French legation of the legation to Berlin)	fine	1	1820
21.	Zietten, *général* (General)	fine	1?	1816
Russia				
22.	*Empereur* Alexandre (Emperor)	2nd print	1	1808-1816
23.	*Palais de légation française de S^e Petersbourg* (Palace of the French legation to St. Petersburg)	fine	1	1820
Spain				
24.	*Marquis de Talaru, pair de France et ambassadeur du Roi à Madrid* (Marquis...Peer of France and Ambassador of the King in Madrid)	fine	1	1824
Sardinia				
25.	*S.M. le Roi de Sardaigne* (H. M. the King of Sardinia)	1st print	1	1815
Sweden				
26.	*Roi de Suède et de Norvège* (King of Sweden and of Norway)	?	1	1822
U.S.A.				
27.	de Neuville, Hyde, *ministre plénipotentiaire aux états unis* (Plenipotentiary Minister)	fine	1	1820
28.	Poletica, *envoyé extraordinare de Russie aux états unis d'amérique* (Special envoy of Russia to the United States of America)	fine	1	1822

Figure 1. The frontispiece of the first edition of the Description. Published with permission from Benedikt Taschen.

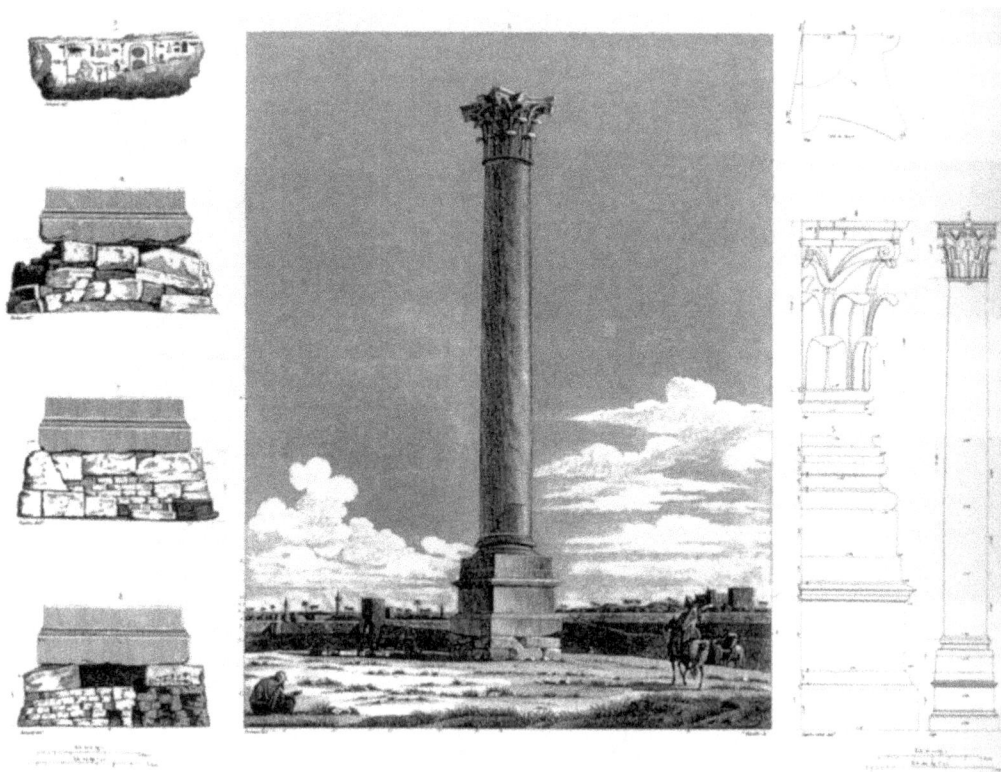

Figure 2. Pompey's Pillar: Alexandria was the northernmost limit of Napoleon's expedition. Published with permission from Benedikt Taschen.

Figure 3. Philae Temple: the southernmost limit of the French expedition's travels. Published with permission from Benedikt Taschen.

Cited works

Baring, T.
1838 *A Bibliographical Account and Collation of* La Description de L'Égypte, *presented to the Library of the London Institution by Sir Thomas Baring, Baronet, President: with a list of other donations made to that establishment from April 1837 to April 1838.* London: Not Published.

Beacour, F., Y. Laissus and C. Orgogozo
1989 *La découverte de l'Égypte.* Paris: Flammarion.

Bidwell, R.
1994 'Introduction', in R. Heron, *Travels Through Arabia and Other Countries in the East, performed by M. Niebuhr* II. Reading: Garnet Publishing.

Bourienne, F.
1830 *Private Memoirs of Napoleon Bonaparte during the periods of the Directory, the Consulate, and the Empire.* London: Henry Colburn and Richard Bentley.

Bret, P. (ed.)
1999 *L'expédition d'Égypte, une entreprise des Lumières 1798-1801.* Paris: Technique & Documentation.

Brunet, J. Ch.
1834 *Nouvelles recherches bibliographiques pour servir le supplément au manuel du libraire et de l'amateur de livres* I. Paris: Silvestre.

Buhl M.-L., E. Dal and T. H. Colding
1986 *The Danish Naval Officer Frederik Ludvig Norden.* Copenhagen: The Royal Danish Academy of Sciences and Letters.

Ceram, C. W.
1954 *Gods, Graves and Scholars: the Story of Archaeology.* London: Victor Gollancz and Sidgwick and Jackson.

Clément, R.
1960 *Les Français d'Égypte aux XVII et XVIII siècles.* Cairo: IFAO.

Dewachter, M. and C. C. Gillispie
1987 *Monuments of Egypt, the Napoleonic Edition, the Complete Archaeological Plates from* la Description de l'Égypte. New Jersey: Princeton Architectural Press.

Dhombres, N. and J. Dhombres
1989 *Naissance d'un pouvoir : sciences et savants en France (1793-1824).* Paris: Éditions Payot.

Fourier, J. B.
1809 'Préface Historique', in *La Description de l'Égypte.* Paris: Imprimerie Impériale.

Guémard, G.
1928 'Les Orientalistes de l'Armée d'Orient', in *Revue de l'Histoire des Colonies Françaises.* March-April: 129-50.

Heron, R.
1792 *Travels Through Arabia and Other Countries in the East, performed by M. Niebuhr* I. Edinburgh: G. Mundie.

Kalfatovic, M. R.
1992 *Nile Notes of a Howadji: a bibliography of travelers' tales from Egypt, from the earliest time to 1918.* London: The Scarecrow Press Inc.

Laissus, Y.
1973 'Description de l'Égypte, bilan scientifique d'une expédition militaire', in G. Bonnin (ed.), *L'Art du livre à l'Imprimerie Nationale.* Paris: Imprimerie Nationale.

Laurens, H.
1987 *Les origines intellectuelles de l'expédition de l'Égypte : L'orientalisme islamisant en France (1698-1798).* Istanbul: Isis Yayimcilik Ltd.
1990 *Le royaume impossible, la France et la genèse du monde arabe.* Paris: Armand Colin Éditeur.

Leclant, J.
1999 'L'égyptologie avant l'expédition d'Égypte', in P. Bret (ed.) *L'expédition d'Égypte, une entreprise des Lumières 1798-1801.* Paris: Technique & Documentation, 121-8.

Le Mascrier, J. B.
1735 *Description de l'Égypte, contenant plusieurs remarques curieuses sur la géographie ancienne et moderne de ce païs, sur ces monumens anciens, sur les moeurs, les coûtumes, & la religion des habitans, sur le gouvernement & le commerce, sur les animaux, les arbres, les plantes &c.* Paris: Louis Genneau.

MF/NAF Series
1802-27 *Délibérations de la Commission chargée de diriger l'exécution de l'Ouvrage sur l'Égypte.* Stored in Paris' Bibliothèque Nationale.

Norden, F. L.
1757 *Travels in Egypt and Nubia.* Trans. P. Templeman. London: L. Davies and C. Reymers.

Pinault-Sørensen, M.
1999 'Du dessin d'artiste ou d'ingénieur au dessin archéologique', in P. Bret (ed.), *L'expédition d'Égypte, une entreprise des Lumières 1798-1801.* Paris: Technique & Documentation, 157-76.

Piussi, A.
1999 'Les menottes d'or du patronage napoléonien: le frontispice de la Description de l'Égypte. Hommage à Dutertre, Balzac et Cécile', in P. Bret (ed.), *L'expédition d'Égypte, une enterprise des Lumières 1798-1801.* Paris: Technique & Documentation, 307-25.

Pococke, R.
1743 *A Description of the East, and some other countries.* London: W. Bowyer.

Reybaud, L.
1830-36 *Histoire scientifique et militaire de l'expédition française en Égypte* I. Paris: A.-J. Dénain et Delamare.

Savary, C. E.
1787 *Letters on Egypt, with a parallel between the manners of ancient and modern inhabitants, the present state, the commerce, the agriculture, and government of that country; and an account of the Descent of St. Lewis at Damietta: extracted from Joinville, and Arabian authors.* 2 Volumes. Dublin: Luke White.

Volney, C. F. Comte de.

1787 *Voyage en Syrie et en Égypte, pendant les années 1783, 1784 et 1785, avec deux cartes géographiques & deux planches gravées, représentant les ruines du Temple du Soleil à Balbek, & celles de la ville de Palmyre dans le Désert de Syrie*. Paris: Volland.

The Arrival of the Horse in Egypt: New Approaches and a Hypothesis

Miriam Bibby

The study of the use of the horse and chariot in the ancient world, and during the second millennium BC in particular, offers the opportunity to observe technological change and innovation.[1] Examining the arrival of this piece of advanced and complex technology in Egypt can give an insight into how ancient, well-established societies coped with change. In the case of New Kingdom Egypt (1550-1069 BC) this might be described as a highly successful integration. The ancient Egyptians can be viewed as a technically innovative society, but Egyptians were not involved in the early stages of chariot development or horse training. Is the arrival of the horse connected in any way to population movements into Egypt and is there a link with the Hyksos?

The use of a pair of horses (as was usual in the ancient world, rather than a single horse) with chariot can be viewed as a specific technological achievement or advance and may be seen as an 'entity' separate from the use of other equids and vehicles, as will be outlined below. Therefore it is important to distinguish between the different types of equid and vehicle and to be able to clearly identify the different types of equid skeletal remains when they are discovered at various sites.

The use of horses (as distinct from other equids) with the relatively light, flexible chariot represents technological progress for the following reasons: the equids (and bovids) previously used were slower, less tractable and/or unable to reproduce. The vehicles, in the early stages of the use of the wheel and draught technology, were heavier, slower and more cumbersome. The swiftness, tractability and reproductive capacity of the horse and the corresponding development of the chariot brought about 'a technological innovation'.[2]

A history of the development of harnessing systems and the types of animal used in Mesopotamia has been well documented for many decades.[3] This evidence has been described in detail by commentators such as Littauer and Crouwel,[4] whose comprehensive work still stands as the major exegesis of the development and spread of vehicle technology in the Middle East during the second millennium BC.

To summarise, early vehicles were first drawn by bovids,[5] using a yoke fastened to the horns and subsequently by equid hybrids of ass and onager (the wild desert ass), which were probably superseded by hybrids of horse and ass before the use of horses and chariot.[6] Equid hybrids, crosses of members of the family *Equidae* (such as the mule, the offspring of a male donkey and a female horse), are almost invariably infertile. At each stage, as the draught animal changed, corresponding advances in vehicle technology took place. However, the traction system at each stage shows its origins in bovid draught, being developmentally descended from the yoke.[7] Raising and training draught animals and developing vehicular technology was an expensive and time-consuming investment and is therefore likely to be representative of high status.

Although the precise location of the first use of the horse and chariot is still open to discussion, there is a well-documented history for at least one part of the ancient world, supported by both archaeological and linguistic evidence, suggestive of a period of technological development regarding vehicles and draught animals. In Sumer, for instance, bovid draught was superseded by draught using hybrids of donkey (ass) and the onager, as indicated by records from sites in that area.[8] From 2050 BC, the horse (*Equus caballus*) is attested at Ur III,[9] being identified as **anse.zi.zi** and **anse.kur.ra**.[10] Other terms which might indicate the 'equid of the mountains' as the horse was identified, in contrast to the onager, the 'equid of the plains', include **anse.LIBIR** and **anse.DUN.GI**, although experts are divided on this.[11] At no stage of the history is there substantial evidence to suggest that the use of the horse was brought about by an 'invasion' from outside nor is its use associated with the arrival of any group of culturally distinct people.

Where then, did the horse originate and how did it make its entry into history as a draught animal? The first horses (distinguished as such from other equids using methodology which will subsequently be

---

[1] Shaw 2001, 59-71.
[2] Piggott 1983, 32.
[3] Säve-Söderbergh 1951, 59.
[4] Littauer and Crouwel 1979, passim.

[5] ibid. 19.
[6] Postgate 1986, 198.
[7] Littauer and Crouwel 1979, 19, 60-1.
[8] Zarins 1986, 188-189.
[9] Postgate 1986, 196.
[10] ibid. 196.
[11] ibid. 196.

described), to be controlled by the use of a bit, and, it is further argued, to be ridden, are identifiable at sites north of the Black Sea in about 4000 BC.[12] This provides a chronological and geographical starting point for the exchange and trade of horses in the ancient world.

Equids in the Ancient World,[13] the proceedings of a conference held at Tübingen in the 1980s summarised research by specialists investigating equid skeletal remains over the last thirty years and more. Furthermore, investigations at various ancient sites at which these remains have been discovered are outlined therein. A useful development from work done by some of the researchers in the field[14] is a methodology to identify and distinguish different equids such as horse (*Equus caballus*), ass (*Equus asinus* [*asinus*]), onager (*Equus hemionus*) and the hybrids produced from interbreeding these equids. This methodology is based on differences in dentition and bone shape and size between the different animals.

By 2000 BC horse skeletal remains occur at Godin Tepe, situated on a trade route through the Zagros Mountains;[15] and horse skeletal remains at Tal e Malyan, in Southern Iraq, have been dated to the same period.[16] Tal e Malyan appears to have been a regional capital of the kingdom of Elam, and Zeder, the investigator of the significant quantities of equid remains there (identified as *Equus caballus*, horse), described the building in which most of these remains were found as 'a terminus for long distance exchange'.[17] Further, Zeder argued that without the status suggested by the remains of horses, this site would have been 'a backwater Elamite outpost'.[18] Trade is therefore presumably stimulated by the arrival of horses at this site.

In western Asia and Syria, quantities of horse bones from sites such as Hayaz Höyuk and Deir Alla suggest a development of the horse trade at a slightly later period.[19] This may be of significance to the arrival of the horse in the Delta of Egypt, and subsequently its importation into Upper Egypt, since there is further equine evidence from Arad in Syria which had an ancient trade connection with Egypt.[20]

I therefore suggest that there is both archaeological and linguistic evidence from the ancient world to support the view that the principal method of acquisition of horses for use with vehicles – in particular chariots – was by identifiable trade or exchange methods. To reinforce this, it is suggested by Anthony that in the north of Europe, the Bell Beaker people may have been responsible for spreading the use of the horse, via commerce.[21] It could be argued that this might represent a group of traders or it might simply represent co-related trade items. However, all the evidence relating to horses and chariots suggests it would be desirable to acquire this advanced technology.

With regard to Egypt, the method by which horses arrived is not as clear. It is generally thought that there is some connection between the Hyksos and the introduction of the horse into Egypt.[22] The most extreme form of belief in the Hyksos as having a particular association with horses and chariots, to the extent that they were an intrinsically warlike and equestrian society, is nowadays confined mainly to novels about ancient Egypt and is not upheld by the majority of Egyptologists. However, without alternative suggestions or proposals it will continue to be misunderstood by those who are not specialists in the subject[23] and therefore it is important that the relationship between the Hyksos and the arrival of horses in Egypt is examined in as much detail as possible.

The basis of any lingering view that the Hyksos were responsible for the introduction of the horse may be traced back to the work of Professor W. M. F. Petrie at Tell el-Ajjul, where he discovered some remarkable interments containing the skeletal remains of equids and humans.[24] In his excavation report it is unequivocally stated that the burials with the horses 'clearly belong to the Hyksos, who introduced the horse to the west'.[25] The Hyksos were at that point viewed as an identifiable group of invaders from the Caucasus. Tell el-Ajjul could, from that perspective, be viewed as being en route to Egypt.

Säve-Söderbergh first pointed out that the Tell el-Ajjul interments are of late date within the Hyksos Period.[26] These equids, whether 'Hyksos horses' or not, would not necessarily therefore provide useful information regarding the earliest horses in Egypt. With regard to

---

[12] Anthony 1991, 250-277; Anthony 1994, 185-95.
[13] Meadow and Uerpmann (eds) 1986 and 1991.
[14] Eisenmann 1986, 67-116; Eisenmann and Beckouche 1986, 117-163.
[15] Gilbert 1986, 75-122.
[16] Zeder 1986, 366-412.
[17] ibid. 406.
[18] ibid. 406.
[19] Buitenhuis 1991, 34-61.
[20] Stevenson Smith 1965, 6.

[21] Anthony 1991, 273.
[22] Bourriau 2000, 215.
[23] Hartley-Edwards 1987, 60.
[24] Petrie 1921, 3-4, 16.
[25] ibid. 3.
[26] Säve-Söderbergh 1951, 59-60.

this, the earliest horses so far known are represented by remains from Tell el Kebir dating to the eighteenth century BC.[27] Säve-Söderbergh also deconstructed various Hyksos attributes as identified by earlier commentators including views on them as being of 'Aryan' origin.[28] A brief commentary was also provided in his paper on the development of draught elsewhere in the ancient world along with the suggestion that the Tell el-Ajjul equids represented both horses and asses.[29]

If the Hyksos were truly invaders of Egypt it would either have to be assumed that they invaded with horses, or that they subsequently acquired them. If the Hyksos acquired horses subsequent to their 'invasion' or arrival, the use of horses could have played no role in the 'invasion'. Tell el-Ajjul, if dated correctly, cannot represent a stage in any 'invasion' of the west by the Hyksos using horses since skeletal remains of horses in the Delta now predate this and the Tell el-Ajjul interments post-date the arrival of the Hyksos in the Delta.

Further, since the methodology to identify equid types was only developed in the latter half of the twentieth century, it was obviously not available during the 1920's excavation of Tell el-Ajjul and it cannot be stated with absolute certainty that the equids are all horses, thus supporting Säve-Söderbergh's view. Whether or not Tell el-Ajjul was correctly identified as a 'Hyksos' site depends upon applying to it a definitive definition of a 'Hyksos site'. Moreover, even if the equids were proven to be horses and Tell el-Ajjul proven to be a Hyksos site, it is not necessarily the case that the individuals in the interments represent 'Hyksos' individuals, however they are to be defined.

Research by Wapnish at Tell Jemmeh,[30] near Tell el-Ajjul, where equid burials have been found, has led to the conclusion that '[A] new date from Mesopotamia confirming the presence of domesticated horse as early as 2300 BC, and especially the presence of domesticated horse in the Negev in the fourth millennium BC, leads me to believe that it is only a matter of time until earlier osteological evidence for the domestic horse in Egypt is found as well.'[31] Wapnish did not link the horse, or the arrival of the horse, with a particular cultural entity, arguing that the inhumation of horses, onagers and donkeys was a region-wide phenomenon,[32] although she further argued that the juvenile equid of Tell Jemmeh may be 'a neonatal foundation sacrifice'[33] thus offering parallels with the Tell el-Ajjul equids which, it was suggested by Petrie, were Hyksos sacrifices, although not neonatal equids.[34] The latest investigation into the one surviving equid skull from Tell el-Ajjul (cited as Gaza in the piece) simply confirms its situation within the Hyksos Period, and identifies it as a horse.[35] Therefore the latest investigations into equid remains in the vicinity of Tell el-Ajjul do not provide particular evidence to suggest identification with the 'Hyksos'.

I would argue, therefore, that a particular connection between the Hyksos and horses in the sense of Hyksos society having specialist equine knowledge and experience prior to arrival in Egypt does not exist. However, that the Hyksos while in Egypt had horses is not in question. In looking to Avaris for enlightenment, the archaeological evidence so far is limited, since firm evidence for horses (and chariots) at the site is not extensive.[36]

Further knowledge of how, when and by what method horses were exchanged in the ancient world is dependent upon continuing to identify their remains, as distinct from those of other equids, with certainty. Often this creates anomalies in the pattern of exchange suggested in this paper and so there is still scope for research. One of the most interesting discoveries made in recent years is that of horses at Shiqmim in the Negev, arguably used for draught, and dated to the fourth millennium BC.[37] Other anomalies remain, such as a definite horse from an early Algerian site[38] and some extremely early remains identified as domesticated horse in Anatolia.[39]

The following hypothesis is proposed: in order to successfully breed and raise horses, good grazing is required. Horses can therefore be bred or raised wherever this is available, within a settled or semi-nomadic way of life, and a source of supply is not constrained to any particular part of the ancient world. Once horses have reached a certain age, they are trained and become working animals (as distinct from breeding stock or young animals). They are then useful, trained animals which may be used by the owner or exchanged for other items. Within the

[27] Anon. Egyptian Archaeology (news item) 1994, 28.
[28] Säve-Söderbergh 1951, 53-71.
[29] ibid. 59.
[30] Wapnish 1997, 335-68.
[31] Wapnish 1997, 355.

[32] ibid. 360.
[33] ibid. 358.
[34] Petrie 1921, 3.
[35] Clutton-Brock and Gowlett 1991, 10.
[36] Boessneck and von den Driesch, 1992, 24-5.
[37] Grigson 1993, 645-55.
[38] Groves 1986, 47.
[39] Bökönyi 1991, 123-31.

ancient world, it is most likely that horses were either 'crown' or 'state' resources, although it is possible that at least some of the breeding activity was carried out by non-royal owners. Horses may be taken to 'exchange centres' by independent traders or, in the ancient world, representatives of crown or state. Textual and archaeological evidence for this type of exchange may be limited, particularly with regard to breeding and raising young horses and is largely dependent upon record keeping of such activities since buildings such as stabling may not be required.

Trade transmission methods can therefore be viewed as resulting and extending from a chain of production involving specialists: breeders, trainers, and horse traders for example, not to mention chariot manufacturers. To this might be added the practice of exchanging gifts of high status directly between rulers, a recognised method of acquiring novel items throughout history.

During the second millennium BC, the growth and apparent success of large acreage sites in Palestine and Syria (such as Gaza, Qatna and Hazor),[40] might be linked to the spread of horse and chariotry technology, with associated weaponry. Horses and chariots in particular would require large areas for testing.

The entry of the horse into the Delta is a different matter to the entry of the horse into Upper Egypt, which will not be discussed in depth in this paper. In this context, Shaw argues that rather than providing an example of technological innovation, as is sometimes assumed, the Hyksos 'may have represented a significant barrier between the Egyptians and access to more sophisticated weapons such as chariots, composite bows and body-armour'.[41] Texts of the early New Kingdom might therefore be viewed in the light of exclusion of the inhabitants of Upper Egypt from a developing round of exchange including the exchange of horses and chariots via trade and gift-giving, resulting in a desire to participate carried out, if necessary, by aggressive means. The effect of the integration of new technology on the Egyptian economy seems to have been good, and it is the Eighteenth Dynasty New Kingdom vision that Egyptology has inherited: an aggressive view of the Hyksos as invaders who needed to be expelled from Egypt. The evidence is not suggestive of an invasion of the Hyksos by chariot; the horse and chariot were therefore not fundamental in their arrival in Egypt.

A number of conclusions might be drawn from recent researches into the identification of equid remains in the ancient world. Firstly, the horse has been used historically as an indicator of population change, since the use of the horse and chariot is an identifiable phenomenon of technological innovation in the ancient world. It makes its entry as a fully-fledged entity into societies that had no previous experience of it and might therefore be incorrectly seen as the product of an aggressive invasion. While this might be a legitimate interpretation of its arrival into non-literate or pre-literate societies where textual material does not exist or is the work of observers from another society, evidence now suggests the unreliability of this approach to the horse and chariot. It is far more likely that the normal transmission methods were by trade and status gift-giving. The horse and chariot is simply another artefact, albeit a highly complex and dramatic one, but it should no more be viewed as indicating the arrival of foreign individuals than should a piece of 'foreign' pottery. Equestrian skills could be acquired by anyone with the application and desire to acquire them. Egypt provides a unique opportunity to test this alternative theory.

Secondly, while it might be argued that a general underlying geographical and chronological pattern with regard to the exchange of horses in the ancient world is visible, with an ultimate source for horses in the region of the Black Sea, the horse and chariot was also a highly desirable status item which would be acquired by, mainly royal, individuals with authority, influence and wealth throughout the ancient world.

Thirdly, the use of chariotry seems, in all societies in which it occurred, to have been confined to a particular class in the upper or military levels of society; indeed a new class may have emerged as a result of it, from existing social groups. This does not necessarily represent an apparently culturally discrete phenomenon such as the 'Maryannu',[42] even though the term 'Maryannu' certainly occurs in specific Egyptian texts, in a context of war and the taking of prisoners.[43] However, it might be argued that the use of the horse and chariot, when acquired by various societies within the Middle East, and later, in Europe, promoted the development of such a class, due to particular requirements in handling a chariot, a possible topic for future research. It is perfectly possible for two groups of people to be culturally similar, perhaps sharing a common language, but for one of those groups to have horses and the other not.

---

[40] Redford 1992, 83.
[41] Shaw 2001, 69.

[42] Wilhelm 1994, 18.
[43] Lichtheim 1976, 32.

Conversely, the fact that two groups of people have access to horses should not mean that they are immediately identified as being culturally similar in other ways, if further evidence is scarce. To use a modern analogy for the 'chariot class': air force pilots from different nation states may be linguistically and ethnically diverse, but they may wear similar uniforms, fly the same planes and have the same skills.

Finally, a particular connection between the Hyksos and the arrival of the horse in the Delta of Egypt is not proven. General belief that there was a connection can provide a particular impression of the Hyksos that is not necessarily accurate. Horses, and chariots, are most likely to have been transmitted or exchanged via trade and status gift-giving rather than brought by invasion or population movements.

Cited works

Anthony, D. W.
1991 'The Domestication of the Horse' in R. Meadow and H.-P. Uerpmann (eds), *Equids in the Ancient World* II. Wiesbaden: Beihefte zum Tübinger Atlas des Vorderen Orients Reihe A 19/2, 250-77.

Anthony, D. W.
1994 'The Earliest Horseback Riders and Indo-European Origins: New Evidence from the Steppes', in B Hänsel and S. Zimmer (eds) *Die Indogermanen und das Pferd, Akten des Internationalen interdisziplinaren Kolloquiums Freie Universität Berlin*. Budapest: Archaeolingua, 185-96.

Bökönyi, S.
1991 'Late Chalcolithic Horses in Anatolia', in R. Meadow and H.-P. Uerpmann (eds), *Equids in the Ancient World* II. Wiesbaden: Beihefte zum Tübinger Atlas des Vorderen Orients Reihe A 19/2, 123-31.

Bourriau, J.
2000 'The Second Intermediate Period', in I. Shaw (ed.), *The Oxford History of Ancient Egypt*. Oxford: Oxford University Press, 184-217.

Boessneck, J. and A. von den Driesch
1992 *Tell el-Dab'a VII: Tiere und historische Umwelt im Nordost-Delta im 2. Jahrtausend v. Chr. anhand der Knochenfunde der Ausgrabungen 1975-1986*. Vienna: Verlag der Österreichischen Akademie der Wissenschaften; Untersuchungen der Zweigstelle Kairo des Österreichischen Ärchäologischen Institutes 10.

Buitenhuis, H.
1991 'Some Equid remains from South Turkey, North Syria and Jordan', in R. Meadow and H.-P.

Uerpmann (eds), *Equids in the Ancient World* II. Wiesbaden: Beihefte zum Tübinger Atlas des Vorderen Orients Reihe A 19/2, 34-61.

Clutton-Brock, J. and J. Gowlett
1991 'Early Domestic Equids in Egypt and Western Asia: an additional note', in R. Meadow and H.-P. Uerpmann (eds), *Equids in the Ancient World* II. Wiesbaden: Beihefte zum Tübinger Atlas des Vorderen Orients Reihe A 19/2, 10.

Eisenmann, V.
1986 'Comparative Osteology of Modern and Fossil Horses, Half-asses and Asses', in R. Meadow and H.-P. Uerpmann (eds), *Equids in the Ancient World* I. Wiesbaden: Beihefte zum Tübinger Atlas des Vorderen Orients Reihe A 19/1, 67-116.

Eisenmann, V. and S. Beckouche
1986 'Identification and Discrimination of Metapodials from Pleistocene and modern *Equus*, Wild and Domesticated' in R. Meadow and H.-P. Uerpmann (eds), *Equids in the Ancient World* I. Wiesbaden: Beihefte zum Tübinger Atlas des Vorderen Orients Reihe A 19/1, 117-63.

Gilbert, A. S.
1986 'Equid remains from Godin Tepe, Western Iran: an interim summary and interpretation with notes on the introduction of the horse into Southwest Asia', 'Identification and Discrimination of Metapodials from Pleistocene and modern *Equus*, Wild and Domesticated' in R. Meadow and H.-P. Uerpmann (eds), *Equids in the Ancient World* I. Wiesbaden: Beihefte zum Tübinger Atlas des Vorderen Orients Reihe A 19/1, 75-122.

Grigson, C.
1993 'The Earliest Domestic Horses in the Levant? – New Finds from the Fourth Millennium of the Negev', *Journal of Archaeological Science* 20: 645-55.

Hartley-Edwards, E.
1987 Horses: *Their Role in the History of Man*. London: Willow Books.

Lichtheim, M.
1976 *Ancient Egyptian Literature* II: *The New Kingdom*. Berkeley: University of California Press.

Littauer, M. and J. H. Crouwel
1979 *Wheeled Vehicles and Ridden Animals in the Ancient Near East*. Leiden and Cologne: E. J. Brill.

Meadow, R. and H.-P. Uerpmann (eds)
1986 *Equids in the Ancient World* I. Wiesbaden: Beihefte zum Tübinger Atlas des Vorderen Orients Reihe A 19/1.

Meadow, R. and H.-P. Uerpmann (eds)
1991 *Equids in the Ancient World* II. Wiesbaden: Beihefte zum Tübinger Atlas des Vorderen Orients Reihe A 19/2.

Petrie, W. M. F.
1921 *Ancient Gaza* I: *Tell el Ajjul*. London: British

School of Archaeology in Egypt aided by New York University (BSAE LIII).

Piggott, S.

1983   *The Earliest Wheeled Transport*. London: Cornell University Press.

Postgate, J. N.

1986 'The Equids of Sumer, again', in R. Meadow and H.-P. Uerpmann (eds), *Equids in the Ancient World* I. Wiesbaden: Beihefte zum Tübinger Atlas des Vorderen Orients Reihe A 19/1, 198.

Redford, D.

1992 *Egypt, Canaan and Israel in Ancient Times*. Princeton: Princeton University Press.

Säve-Söderbergh, T.

1951   'The Hyksos Rule in Egypt', *JEA* 37: 53-71.

Shaw I.

2001   'Egyptians, Hyksos and Military Technology: Causes, Effects or Catalysts?' in A. J. Shortland (ed.), *The Social Context of Technological Change: Egypt and the Near East 1650-1550 BC*. Oxford: Oxbow.

Stevenson Smith, W.

1965 *Interconnections in the Ancient Near East: a Study of the Arts of Egypt, the Aegean, and Western Asia*. New Haven: Yale University Press.

Wapnish, P.

1997 'Middle Bronze Age Equid Burials at Tell Jemmeh and a re-examination of a Purportedly "Hyksos" practice' in E. D. Oren (ed.), *The Hyksos: New Historical and Archaeological Perspectives*. Philadelphia: University Museum, University of Pennsylvania; University Museum Monograph 96, 335-68.

Wilhelm, G.

1994 *The Hurrians*, trans. J. Barnes. Warminster: Aris and Philips; Ancient Near East Series.

Zarins, J.

1986 'Equids Associated with Human Burials in the Third Millennium' in R. Meadow and H.-P. Uerpmann (eds), *Equids in the Ancient World* I. Wiesbaden: Beihefte zum Tübinger Atlas des Vorderen Orients Reihe A 19/1, 189.

Zeder, M.

1986 'The Equid Remains from Tal-e Malyan, Southern Iraq' in R. Meadow and H.-P. Uerpmann (eds), *Equids in the Ancient World* I. Wiesbaden: Beihefte zum Tübinger Atlas des Vorderen Orients Reihe A 19/1, 366-412.

Aspects of the Hyksos' Role in Egyptian Society from the Artistic Evidence

Charlotte Booth

Introduction

The Hyksos are best known from the Second Intermediate Period when they ruled Egypt from their capital in the Delta. Manetho would have us believe that 'from regions of the East, invaders of obscure race marched in confidence of victory against our land... ...by main force they took it without striking a blow'.[1]

Archaeological evidence shows that there was a large Canaanite population in the Delta prior to this period, but the drastic change of pottery styles suggests an invasion or somewhat violent change of power.[2] At the height of Hyksos rule, Avaris had doubled in size from the settlement of the Thirteenth Dynasty.[3] The sudden expansion of the settlement at Avaris at the start of Hyksos rule indicates a sudden influx of people into the area. Ryholt believes this supports the theory of an invasion in this period,[4] although it seems likely that any new capital would draw a large number of people due to the probability of it being the most prosperous area.

Background

Some Asiatics in the Middle Kingdom held positions of authority and therefore were not really 'the Barbarians'[5] that New Kingdom texts would indicate. A number of stelae and inscriptions show officials with Asiatic names, or with Egyptian names, but who name their Asiatic parents.[6] Asiatic children, captured as spoils of war, were sometimes trained in Egypt to be palace administrators, scribes, magicians or soldiers for the army.

The 'Admonitions of Ipuwer',[7] although thought to record the First Intermediate Period, gives some indication of the unrest that could have existed at the time of the Second Intermediate Period. The 'Admonitions' tell of chaos that has gripped the land, with famine, looting and riots and also makes reference to a foreign tribe coming into Egypt. This chaos described could have been replicated in the Second Intermediate Period as the Middle Kingdom collapsed. A plague is also described in the 'Admonitions' (2,5-6) 'throughout the land' resulting in 'death in abundance'. Although this could be metaphorical for the disruption and chaos that was spreading through the land, there is evidence from Tell el Dab'a of an epidemic of the 'Canaanite illness', generally thought to be the bubonic plague,[8] in the late Thirteenth Dynasty which was thought to have originated within Asiatic tribes. The kings of the Thirteenth Dynasty moved the capital from Lisht, just south of Memphis, to Thebes in 1685 BC[9] possibly in an attempt to calm the political unrest, or as a precaution against the epidemic.

However, even before the site at Lisht had been abandoned in favour of Thebes, there had already been some division of power. The so-called Fourteenth Dynasty was ruling the Delta area at the same time as the Thirteenth Dynasty. The first king of this dynasty was Sheshi who is thought to have reigned for 40 years followed by his son Nehesy who reigned for a year.[10] Limestone door-jambs of Nehesy discovered at Tell el Dab'a and other inscribed fragments found at Tell el Habua, Tanis and Tell el Muqdam (places where no Thirteenth Dynasty monuments have as yet been found), would suggest Fourteenth Dynasty power was limited to the Eastern Delta.[11] This apparent abandonment of the Northern regions, after the Thirteenth Dynasty moved to Thebes, left these areas open to internal power struggles which eventually resulted in the Hyksos being accepted as the rulers of Lower Egypt.

Regardless of this internal struggle the new Hyksos rulers did not seem to fear outside attack. A reinforced surrounding wall at Avaris was not built until near the end of the period (1570-1540 BC) at a time when they would have felt threatened by the Theban dynasties, who at this time seem to have been becoming restless with the division of Egypt. At the beginning of the Hyksos rule the division of Egypt would have caused economic problems in both regions by cutting access to trade routes which would have been used regularly during the Middle Kingdom. This would have taken both areas some time to overcome, hence the delay in the Theban Dynasties retaliating against the foreign rulers.

---

[1] Waddel 1940, 79.
[2] Ryholt 1997, 303.
[3] Bourriau 2000, 193.
[4] Ryholt 1997, 303.
[5] Breasted 1906, 125.
[6] The body of evidence was collected by Kitchen 1991, 87-90.
[7] Gardiner 1909.

[8] Goedicke 1986, 94.
[9] Bourriau 2000, 185.
[10] Ryholt 1997, 252.
[11] Bourriau 2000, 190.

Unfortunately the surviving narrative texts from this period are written by Egyptians, following a certain protocol in style, and project the image of the 'mighty' Egyptians suppressing 'barbaric' foreigners. As no narrative texts written by the Hyksos have survived, a small number of artistic representations and archaeological evidence can help to determine the real role they played within Egyptian society. Four very different images will be discussed here, from varying periods and areas. Such a small data set does not permit strong conclusions but I hope to raise some questions regarding the accuracy of the Egyptian propagandistic texts.

The evidence

The earliest piece to be discussed is a relief from tomb three at Beni Hasan[12] belonging to Khnumhotep, the 'Administrator of the Eastern Desert and the Mayor of Menet-Khufu' from the Twelfth Dynasty (Figure 1). This relief shows a group of twelve Asiatics consisting of eight men, four women, and three servants. They are presenting two gazelles and two donkeys to the deceased Khnumhotep.[13] The men are all shown with thin beards, hooked noses and colourful, patterned garments. The four women are shown in long patterned dresses, anklets and Egyptian-style tri-partite wigs. They all have distinctive hooked noses, common to representations of Asiatics. The leader of this group is the chief Absha who is called ḥqȝ ḫȝswt, which means 'leader of foreign lands' and from which the modern term 'Hyksos' is derived. He is leading a large gazelle and has a more elaborate costume than the others, with a fringe running along the front edge. The Asiatics following behind are seen carrying Asiatic spears, axes and composite bows. They are represented at the same size as the surrounding Egyptians, but are clearly differentiated by the colour of their skin and their bright clothing, in comparison to the Egyptians who are wearing plain loin cloths and have dark skin.

The first of the objects produced by the Hyksos to be discussed here is the head of a twice life-size dignitary statue (Figure 2) found in a chapel adjacent to a Hyksos tomb from Avaris. It has been dated to the late Middle Kingdom or early Second Intermediate Period.[14] This statue has been intentionally damaged, leaving only the hair and part of the face, although this, and the archaeological context, is enough to define the object as Asiatic in origin. When this damage was caused is unknown, which makes it difficult to discern the motivation behind this destruction.

The statue was discovered in the stratum of Tell el Dab'a from the beginning of the Hyksos Period, and has been identified as a Hyksos official.[15] The statue has no parallels in Egypt, the closest parallel being an example discovered in Ebla,[16] and is therefore not thought to be Egyptian in origin. The 'mushroom' hair-style is very similar in style to those in the tomb of Khnumhotep at Beni Hasan, and traces of red paint were found on this part of the statue. The skin shows traces of yellow paint, which was traditional for representations of Asiatics by the Egyptians. This could suggest that the stereotypical imagery used by the Egyptians was accepted by the Asiatics, and therefore could be a realistic representation of them. In an area like Avaris there would have been no need for the Asiatics to try and conform to the stereotypical imagery used by the Egyptians. The numerous non-Egyptian characteristics of this statue would suggest they did not feel the need to conceal their Asiatic origins.

The second figure is an ivory sphinx (Figure 3) found in Abydos tomb 477, and has been dated to the Second Intermediate Period, and clearly shows the face of an Asiatic ruler.[17] The sphinx would originally have been part of the handle of a box. This sphinx has the head of a king wearing the *nemes* head-dress and between his paws is a struggling human figure who resembles an Egyptian with close cropped hair and wearing a plain loin cloth. The sphinx shows Asiatic facial features, seen particularly well in profile, with a large, hooked nose common to other Asiatic representations. As the only known Asiatic rulers of this period were the Hyksos from the Delta region, it is thought to be a representation of one of these rulers.[18] It is possibly Khayan (1621-1581 BC) as he was the first of the Hyksos rulers to conquer Upper Egypt, or at least to adopt the title of 'King of Upper and Lower Egypt'.

The owner of the tomb is unknown but associated finds would suggest he or she was a member of the elite class and the workmanship of the object under discussion strongly supports this. The owner of the sphinx clearly treasured this item since it escaped destruction, and was included amongst the funerary objects. The existence of this sphinx so far south of Avaris could suggest that the support of the Hyksos

---

12 Newberry 1893.
13 Newberry 1893.
14 Bietak 1996, 20.

15 ibid. 20.
16 ibid. 20.
17 Garstang 1928, 46.
18 ibid. 46.

rulers was not limited to the Delta region. As this area of Egypt was under the rule of the Theban Dynasties it suggests there were divided opinions in Upper Egypt amongst the members of the elite regarding the foreign rulers. This further suggests that the propagandistic texts of this period do not necessarily reflect the ideas of the population.

The final figure for discussion is a terracotta head from Memphis (Figure 4) identified by Petrie as a Syrian.[19] It was dated by Petrie as being manufactured between 500-300 BC. The head has short-cropped curly hair, Egyptian style eyes and a large, somewhat hooked nose. The skin shows evidence that it was coloured red and the hair was black. Petrie believed the rounded face to be indicative of a comfortable life and placed him as either a Syrian or Jewish trader. However, the profile of this terracotta head is remarkably similar to Absha from Beni Hasan. The nose is similar in shape although more exaggerated in the Memphis head; the hair style and the thin beard are also similar. These similarities could therefore place this figure as a possible *ḥq3 ḫ3swt* (or 'Hyksos') rather than a Syrian or a Hebrew, even though the facial coloration does not conform to previous stereotypes. This could, however, be due to the very late date of this piece in comparison to the objects discussed above. The reasons for the manufacture of this piece and the identity of its owner are unknown, but the relaxed style and cheery features could suggest it was a caricature or even a portrait of someone in the town. Either way, this figure does not seem to represent a 'barbarian' or a person of 'obscure race' as Manetho described the Hyksos.

Discussion

With such a small number of objects one can only generalise about the acceptance of the Hyksos into Egyptian society. However, the scarcity of negative imagery of the Hyksos could suggest that they were more accepted than the texts would allow us to believe. One example of such negative imagery comes from the temple of Ahmose at Abydos, which shows two Hyksos warriors, one as a captive with a shaved head and stubble beard with a rope around his neck and another wearing a long sleeved fringed garment,[20] similar to that worn by Absha in the Beni Hasan relief. However, the imagery in this temple is completely stereotypical of captured enemies, and therefore can be seen as a product of Egyptian political propaganda. These stereotypical smiting scenes do not differentiate one group of Asiatics from another, and in the Ahmose relief, it is only the accompanying text that identifies them as Hyksos. These stereotypical images do not reflect the feelings of the populace.

Texts dating from after the expulsion of the Hyksos from Egypt were written to reinforce the role the New Kingdom kings played in the maintenance of the Rule of Maat. Convincing the populace that the Hyksos were barbarians, through tales of destruction and looting, ensured the new kings were seen as saviours. These tales would have been circulated verbally through the community, and may have developed into 'myths'. However, if the Asiatics were as mistrusted and hated as the texts would indicate, they would not have been able to rise to positions of authority, and if they did, they would have been discouraged from acknowledging their non-Egyptian origins.

The tomb of Khnumhotep, being so far south, shows that knowledge of Asiatic races was not limited to Lower Egypt. After the Hyksos Period, knowledge and acceptance of the Hyksos went as far south as Abydos, as the ivory sphinx (Figure 3) would suggest. Abydos would have been at that time under the rule of the Theban Dynasties, which could suggest some divided opinion amongst the people of Egypt concerning the rulers of that time.

Two of the four objects discussed are not from Asiatic dominated areas and could have been owned or commissioned by Egyptian or Asiatic people whereas the statue from Avaris is clearly from an Asiatic community, and the terracotta head from Memphis is thought to have originated in what Petrie termed the 'foreign quarter'.[21] Although there is no definite archaeological evidence of a 'foreign quarter' there is much evidence that Memphis during the Ptolemaic Period was a multi-cultural society, where different nationalities lived together whilst maintaining an Egyptian life style. There were a number of temples here dedicated to foreign gods, as well as it being the cult centre of Ptah and the Apis Bull. These foreign deities were gradually absorbed into the Egyptian pantheon.

Memphis was a major port, and the numerous workshops would have meant a large number of foreigners would have been travelling through there. From the representations discussed above it is clear that Asiatics were a familiar aspect of life. The tomb of Khnumhotep shows them in an official aspect as

---

[19] Petrie 1909, 16.
[20] Bourriau 2000, 213.

[21] Petrie 1910, 46.

part of a trading venture, and suggests a relationship between the Egyptians and this group of foreigners. The sphinx from the tomb from Abydos, which does not appear to have other Asiatic characteristics, could suggest that the tomb owner was an Egyptian who was sympathetic towards the Asiatic rulers of this period. The statue found in the Asiatic capital and representing an Asiatic merely shows that they were living here and were living according to their own traditions and culture. The terracotta head is a little more problematic as the craftsman, and audience, is unknown. It does, however, indicate that there was an Asiatic element to the community at Memphis, either living there or at least common enough to be familiar to the craftsman of this object. With such a small group of isolated images no conclusion can be drawn other than that the Egyptians allowed foreigners to settle in Egypt. Even this however, would have been dependant on their ability to abide by the rule of Maat, and become a part of Egyptian society. Anyone who threatened this continuance of peace was mistrusted, but those living within the society were very much viewed as members of Egyptian society regardless of their ethnic origin.

Charlotte Booth
Institute of Archaeology
University College London

Figure 1. Detail of Absha from the Tomb of Khnumhotep. Twelfth Dynasty. Beni Hasan. After Newberry 1893, pl. XXXI.

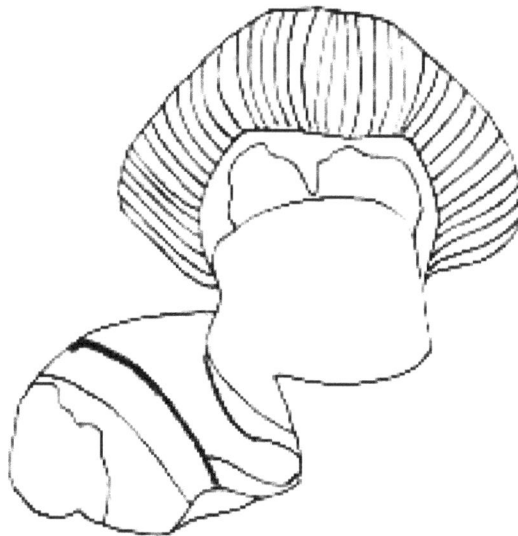

Figure 2. Statue remains from Avaris. After Bietak 1996, fig 17.

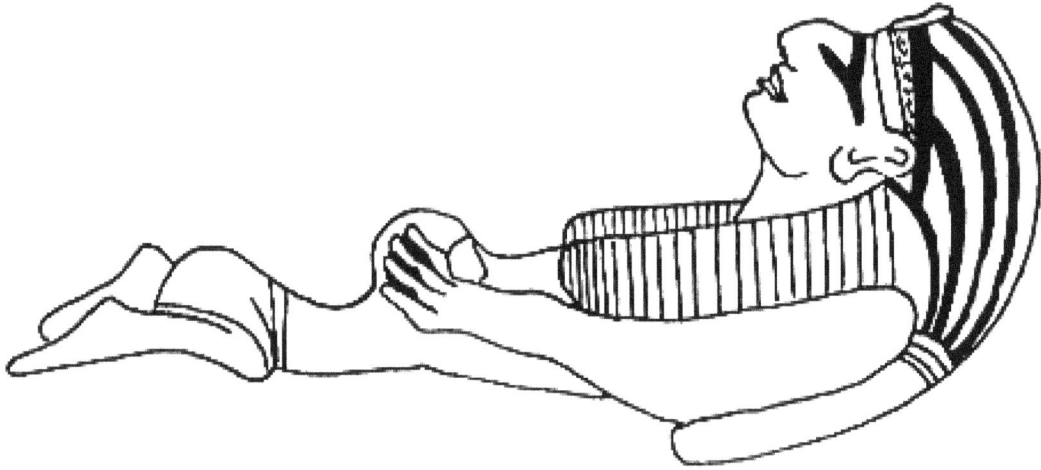

Figure 3. Ivory Sphinx from Abydos, Second Intermediate Period.
British Museum BM 56478. After Garstang 1928, pl. VII.

Figure 4. Terracotta Head from Memphis. Petrie Museum UC 33278. After Petrie 1909, pl. XXXVI.

Cited works

Bietak, M.
1996 *The Capital of the Hyksos: Recent Excavations at Tell el Dab'a.* London: British Museum Press.

Bourriau, J.
2000 'The Second Intermediate Period', in I. Shaw (ed.), *The Oxford History of Ancient Egypt.* Oxford: Oxford University Press: 184-218.

Breasted, J. H.
1906 *Ancient Records of Egypt: Historical Documents from the Earliest to the Persian Conquest.* Chicago: The University of Chicago Press.

Clayton, P. A.
1994 *Chronicle of the Pharaohs: the Reign-by-Reign Record of the Rulers and Dynasties of Ancient Egypt.* London: Thames and Hudson.

Goedicke, H.
1986 *The Quarrel of Apophis and Seqenenrec.* San Antonio: Van Siclen Books.

Gardiner, A. H.
1909 *The Admonitions of an Egyptian Sage: From a Hieratic Papyrus in Leiden (Pap. Leiden 344 Recto).* Leipzig: J. C. Hinrichs.

Garstang, J.
1928 'An Ivory Sphinx From Abydos BM # 56478', *JEA* 14: 46.

Kitchen, K. A.
1991 'Non-Egyptians recorded on Middle Kingdom Stelae in Rio Di Janeiro', in S. Quirke (ed.), *Middle Kingdom Studies.* New Malden: SIA Publishing, 87-90.

Newberry, P. E.
1893 *Beni Hasan* I. London: Kegan Paul, Trench, Trübner and Co, Egypt Exploration Fund; Archaeological Survey of Egypt Memoir 1.

Petrie, W. M. F.
1909 *Memphis* I. London: Bernard Quaritch.

Petrie W. M. F., E. Mackay and G. Wainwright
1910 *Meydum and Memphis* III. London: School of Archaeology in Egypt.

Ryholt, K. S. B.
1997 *The Political Situation in Egypt During the Second Intermediate Period, c. 1800-1550 BC.* Copenhagen: K. S. B. Ryholt and Museum Tusculanum Press.

Waddel, W. G.
1940 *Manetho.* London: W. Heinemann Ltd; Loeb Classical Library.

SOME THOUGHTS ON THE SOCIAL ORGANISATION OF DOCKYARDS DURING THE NEW KINGDOM

Angus Graham

Introduction

The Nile has been described as the major transport and communication artery of ancient Egypt.[1] Furthermore, it is suggested that this use of the Nile was a prominent factor in shaping the economy, political organisation and demography of the country.[2] The boat was an essential feature of the lives of those Egyptians living in the Nile valley and Delta.

This paper discusses the social organisation of the workshops/dockyards that constructed and repaired vessels during the New Kingdom. Dürring has produced an important work discussing not only the materials used to construct vessels, but also those who carried out the work and the organisations in which they operated.[3] It is his view of the organisation of the New Kingdom *königlichen Werft* that provides the stimulus for this paper.

Dürring stated that the New Kingdom royal organisation he proposed is not comparable to that of the *Privatwerft* of the Old Kingdom, which he defined as the dockyard or workshop owned by a private estate (*pr-ḏt*). He argued that the royal or state dockyard of the New Kingdom is defined by the use of the term *pr-ꜥꜣ* or by the link between the treasury (*pr-ḥḏ*) and the dockyard as demonstrated in written communications.[4] I would argue that the royal or state dockyard should include both dockyards with royal designations and temple dockyards. The distinction between temple and state craft workers was more of formal than practical significance as the various institutions and those working in them all performed functions by delegation and acted as components of the state as a whole.[5] It is argued that the various craft workers in the New Kingdom belonged to workshops either in the service of the state or private estates (*pr-ḏt*) and generally did not own or control the materials and tools that they used, and there was therefore little scope for private work in their own time.[6] However, the tomb scenes of the New Kingdom show the tomb owner supervising institutional craft organisations; in the case of the Theban tombs these are the workshops of Amun. This is in contrast to the scenes from the Old and Middle Kingdoms, which depict the tomb owner supervising workers employed in their own household, suggesting that New Kingdom workers were linked to state institutions.[7] Returning to the question of dockyard or boat building workshops specifically, the evidence presented is taken from royal accounts mentioning the dockyards of *prw-nfr* and *ḥry-nfr*, model letters, and from items owned by the titleholder.[8]

As Eyre pointed out any study of the organisation of labour suffers from the partiality and unevenness of the evidence.[9] With this in mind the paper will add to the evidence used by Dürring in order to further the discussion in the hope that this work will be added to or superseded in the future. It is also the aim of the paper to show that the evidence does not support the static picture produced by Dürring for the New Kingdom.

imy-r mḏḥ.w and *imy-r ḥmw.w*

The work of Dürring and other scholars[10] suggests that the title *imy-r mḏḥ.w* was used from the Old

---

[1] Hassan 1997, 54; Kemp and O'Connor 1974, 101. Whilst overland routes through the desert did exist between parts of the Nile, for example the Luxor-Farshût Road (see Darnell and Darnell 1997, 24-6) their use does not appear to have been significant in terms of the movement of people, animals, goods and materials. In the valley itself the dikes and irrigation basins would have hampered the land routes in the floodplain, while the Nile branches in the Delta would have further impeded land routes in this area. Although the desert routes did not suffer from such obstacles, the use of pack animals and of wooden sleds either pulled by humans or oxen could not match the carrying capacity and speed of a boat on the Nile: Eyre 1987a, 11; Hassan 1993, 556; Kemp and O'Connor 1974, 101. Compare estimates of carrying capacity of donkeys, humans and oxen: Arnold 1991, 58, 63-4; Hassan 1993, 565, 566, with that of New Kingdom grain-carrying vessels: Gardiner 1941; Hornell 1943.
[2] Hassan 1993, 556, 559.
[3] Dürring 1995.
[4] Dürring 1995, 199-201. He did not mention the qualification of nswt in the textual evidence, but one presumes it is implicit.

[5] Eyre 1987b, 194.
[6] Drenkhahn 1995, 334. An exception to this notion is the case of the state-employed workers at Deir el-Medina. They used tools and equipment provided by the state for their official work, but also appear to have had their own tools which they used to produce objects for private consumption: Drenkhahn 1995, 335; Eyre 1987b, 175, 199.
[7] Drenkhahn 1995, 333; Drenkhahn 1976, 3, 134; Eyre 1987b, 193.
[8] It should not be ruled out that the small vessels used at a local level in the daily lives of individuals may have been produced and / or repaired at a private level in the spare time of the boat builder. This area of discussion is, however, not within the scope of this paper.
[9] Eyre 1987b, 167.
[10] Drenkhahn 1976, 121; Dürring 1995, 173-184; Wb II, 190,9; Jones 2000, 146 no. 571; Jones 1988, 119 no. 2; Steinmann 1980, 151.

Kingdom to the Middle Kingdom in connection with shipbuilding as well as other woodworking activities.[11] The title appears not to be attested in the context of shipbuilding in the New Kingdom, which suggests that a change occurred in the titles associated with shipyard activities.[12]

Whilst the title *imy-r ḥmw(.w/.t)* is not found in Dürring's New Kingdom organisation, there are, however, examples that may be associated with shipbuilding.[13] One is from the 'timber accounts' of the so-called 'Palace Accounts of Seti I'. It records that Hat, an *imy-r ḥmw.w* 'overseer of craftsmen', received a piece of boat timber for work on a door.[14] Another possible example is in the Golénischeff Onomasticon from the late Twentieth Dynasty.[15] However, the reconstructed title [*imy-r*] *ḥmw wḥr* must remain problematic due to the lacuna and it also relies upon the understanding of the addition of *wḥr(t)* to the title.

The term *wḥrt* has long been recognised as referring to either a dockyard or a boat building shop, or more generally a carpenter's workshop.[16] It certainly appears that the term refers to the more generic meaning for a place where woodworking, including the building of boats, was carried out during the Old Kingdom.[17]

From the Middle Kingdom come some examples with a boat determinative in both administrative and religious contexts.[18] As for the New Kingdom, whilst there appear to be clear instances of the term being used to refer to a dockyard or boat building workshop,[19] there remains a number of examples that have insufficient context to be certain of the meaning of the term.[20] The two examples of the title *imy-r ḥmw* are not clearly from within a boat building context and it seems prudent at this time not to include the title in any organisation of shipbuilding in the New Kingdom.

Werkstoffbeschaffung

Dürring placed some titles of individuals under the heading *Werkstoffbeschaffung* in his scheme.[21] He seemed to be suggesting that these people were supplied with work materials, but not involved in the construction of the hull of the vessel. He included the titles *ḥmw t3r.t*[22] and *ḥmw wrs.w*.[23] A number of other people would have been involved in the

---

[11] An unnamed individual depicted in a boat building scene holds the title in the Sixth Dynasty tomb of Ibi at Deir el-Gebrawi: Davies 1902, pl. XV; Porter and Moss 1934, 243-4. A scene in the tomb of Pepi-ankh at Meir shows the 'overseer of carpenters' Henenit adzing a plank whilst two other men polish (?) a wooden bedstead: Blackman and Apted 1953, 28, pl. 18. The Twelfth Dynasty example in the tomb of Khnumhotep at Beni Hasan (no. 3) shows a man with the title *imy-r mḏḥ.w* adzing wood: Newberry 1893, pl. 29. The context does not definitively connect him to shipbuilding although shipbuilding occurs in the register below.

[12] The term *smsw wḥrt* is another example of changes in titles of those involved in shipbuilding and repair. The term is found in the Old and possibly the Middle Kingdom, but it is not attested after this period. See n. 14 for references and discussion of meaning.

[13] For references to individuals with the title working in different or unspecified labour organisations, see Caminos 1954, 500; Drenkhahn 1976, 83; Steinmann 1980, 141-3; Wb III 84, 85.

[14] Helck 1965, 287 (895); Kitchen 1975, 263,7; Kitchen 1993a, 219: 263,7. For references and discussion of the boat timber, *bnbn*, given to Hat (HAt), see Glanville 1932, 11 n. 10, 34; Jones 1988, 163 no. 48. The so-called 'Palace Accounts' are discussed in Kitchen 1993b, 159-185. Other recipients of timber in these accounts include the 'agent or administrator of the dockyard Menkhet', *rwḏw mnḥt n t3 wḥrt*, Helck 1965, 290 (898); Kitchen 1975, 267,3; Kitchen 1993a, 222: 267,3; Vandorpe 1995, 164.

[15] Gardiner 1947, 215*.

[16] Faulkner 1962, 68; Jones 1988, 203 no. 3; Kemp and O'Connor 1974, 104-5; Lesko 1982, 127.

[17] This is exemplified by the term *smsw wḥrt* 'Elder of the workshop' in a number of Old Kingdom tomb scenes. The individuals who hold this title are found both supervising and being involved in the construction of vessels in tomb scenes, for

example of Ti, Steindorff 1913, taf. 119-120; Wild 1953, pl. 129; Mereruka, Duell 1938, pl. 150; Niankhkhnum and Khnumhotep, Moussa and Altenmüller 1977, Abb 8; and Rahotep, Petrie 1892, pl. XI; all found in the necropoleis of the Old Kingdom royal residences. The same title is also held by individuals supervising the polishing of other wooden items such as couches, Davies 1902, 11, pl. X; and bedsteads, Blackman and Apted 1953, pl. 18; found in tombs at Deir el-Gebrawi and Meir respectively. There is the possibility that this title and others had synchronic differences in their usage according to geographical factors, but further work is needed to clarify this hypothesis.

[18] P. Reisner II, Simpson 1965. Coffin Text 397 in the burial chamber and on the coffin (Cairo 28023) of Hor-hotep, de Buck 1954, V84 T1C; Faulkner 1977, 25.

[19] For example in P. BM 10056, Glanville 1932, 28, and P. Anastasi IV, 8,6, Caminos 1954, 160, 163; Gardiner 1937, 43; Helck 1965, 296 (904). See Drenkhahn 1976, 123 for a definition of the activities occurring.

[20] For example Grandet 1994, 51 n. 203, argued that there is insufficient context in P. Harris I (BM 9999) to propose the translation of *chantiers navals* for the term *wḥrt.w* and prefers *des ateliers de charpentage*; cf. Haring 1997, 174, 202. The juxtaposition of *mnš*-vessels in the lists makes the translation of 'shipyards' plausible.

[21] Dürring 1995, 200 Abb. 71.

[22] P. BM 10056 r. 14, 12-14 relates that the cabin-maker (Hmw TAr.t, lit. craftsman of cabins) Amenhotep son of Sekhmet(?)hetep was supplied with timber to carry out his work, Glanville 1931, 115; Glanville 1932, 20-2, n. 49; Helck 1965, 272 (880). A limestone relief from a Nineteenth Dynasty Memphite tomb shows a scene of work on a vessel deckhouse, Wreszinski 1923, taf. 420.

[23] The title is 'craft worker of oars' or 'oar-maker' Wb I, 364, 3; Wb III, 82, 11; Jones 1988, 121 no. 15; Steinmann 1980, 152; Taylor 2001, 147 no. 1430. The title is found in the model letter so-called 'A Letter of Complaints' - P. Anastasi VI (BM 10245), Caminos 1954, 282; Gardiner 1937, 75. The title is also held by Tuer (*twr*), who is named on his father's stela in the second half of the Eighteenth Dynasty, Spiegelberg 1904, pl. VIII, 13.

completion of vessels.[24] Of these, two of the terms for sculptor, *sꜥnḫ*[25] and *gnw.tj* (or *qs.tj*)[26] appear in P. BM 10056.[27] The 'wood carver' *ḥmw sꜥnḫ* (v. 2/1) is given materials for work on part of the vessel and Nebwahyeb, a *gnwtj* 'sculptor' is mentioned (v. 5/1, v. 5/6) in connection with timber for the *ḏrit*. *ḏrit* is argued to refer to the ship's finial, columns supporting the cabin, or deckhouse wall, all of which may have required the skills of a wood carver or sculptor.[28] They could be added to this group who are supplied with materials, but not involved in the main construction within the organisation of this royal dockyard at Memphis.[29] None of the sources that mention these job titles clearly reveal who distributed the materials to these workers. Further evidence is required in order to clarify whether they received them directly from the dockyard administrators or scribes or perhaps from the *ḥmw wr*, who had received the materials from the administrators.

pr(y)

The title *pr(y)* is found nine times in the Twelfth Dynasty P. Reisner II. The title holder, Nebyot, is thought to have worked in parallel with the stewards (*imy-r pr*), scribes (*sš*) and foremen (*ḥrp*) as an administrative official rather than having associations with carpentry.[30] This is in contrast to the late Twentieth Dynasty appearance of *pr(y)* in P. Lansing 5, 4-6. Here the *pr(y)* is described as doing the toughest of all jobs, working in the fields with his tool-box and returning home with timber in the evening.[31] This must be seen in the context of the text itself, which seeks to criticise all professions except that of the scribe. Erman and Lange argued that it is

difficult to assess the job of the *pry* without knowing what tools they used.[32] The idea that the *pry* was a 'carpenter's assistant' is disputed.[33] Dürring argued that the title must have experienced a change of esteem and importance from the Twelfth to the late Twentieth Dynasty as the title seems to rank below that of *ḥmw* in P. Lansing.[34] The only other example known to this author is in the late Twentieth Dynasty Golénischeff Onamasticon.[35] The title is within a short list of titles that appear related to vessel construction and crew. It is, however, not safe to assume that the rank of *pry* and the other titles can be deduced from their position within the list.[36] It is therefore somewhat misleading to place the *pry* at the bottom of a scheme for the New Kingdom organisation when we have no evidence of when a change in rank and role occurred.

The role of the vizier

The so-called 'Duties of the Vizier',[37] argued to have been composed during the reign of Ahmose,[38] include assigning ships to those who need them.[39] However, van den Boorn[40] believed that these texts should not be seen as simple descriptions of the individual functions carried out by the vizier, but more as a collection of duties with the aim of outlining the position of the vizier as a whole.

There does, however, appear to be a precedent for such duties in the records of Antefoker, the vizier to Senwosret I. P. Reisner II contains three administrative orders, all from Antefoker, that deal with complaints and give orders to ship certain items, have others ready for collection, and also for the delivery of timber to the royal workshop.[41] A Twelfth Dynasty papyrus fragment from el-Lisht appears to

---

[24] Dürring 1995, 197.

[25] See Drenkhahn 1976, 126; Gardiner 1947, 67*; Steinmann 1980, 152.

[26] See Drenkhahn 1976, 62; Gardiner 1947, 66*. Dürring 1995, 107-8 B20, suggests that an example in a boatbuilding tomb scene (TT109) is a unique occurrence or possibly a miswriting of *ḥmw.tj*.

[27] P. BM 10056 is the accounts of a royal dockyard, Perunefer, Glanville 1932, 1931. The dockyard has been interpreted by some scholars as playing a key role in the construction and repair of vessels used in the military campaigns of Thutmose III and Amenhotep II, see for example Säve-Söderbergh 1946, 39; Zayed 1987, 108. However, the mention of military vessels is not in evidence in the text.

[28] Glanville 1932, 23-4 n. 61, 27 n. 81; Helck 1965, 274 (882), 282 (890); Jones 1988, 196 no. 191.

[29] The location of Perunefer is still a matter of debate and while a number of locations in the Delta have been proposed, it seems most likely that it was somewhere in the vicinity of Memphis. For a discussion of the location and references to the range of views see Glanville 1932, 27-30 n. 86; Jeffreys 1996, 292-4; Kamish 1986; Vandorpe 1995, 162-5; Zayed 1987, 89-97.

[30] Simpson 1965, 42.

[31] Caminos 1954, 388-9; Erman and Lange 1925, 58-9.

[32] Erman and Lange 1925, 59.

[33] Gardiner 1947, 215*; Wb I, 526.

[34] Dürring 1995, 188.

[35] Gardiner 1947, 215*.

[36] The 'Onomastica of Amenope' is made up of a number of sources, of which the Golénischeff Onomasticon is one. It is argued that an attempt was made within the opening part of the lists at some sort of order of precedence. However, within the lists of occupations, where we find the mention of the pry, no simple sequence of rank exists: Gardiner 1947, 38; Steinmann 1991, 153.

[37] The texts are found in the Eighteenth Dynasty tombs of Rekhmire (TT 100), his predecessor Amenuser (TT 131) and his successor Amenemopet (TT 29) with a version of the text also known from the tomb of the later vizier Paser (TT 106) from the reign of Ramesses II: Davies 1943a, 88-9.

[38] van den Boorn 1988, 344, 375; cf. van den Boorn 1982, 381.

[39] Davies 1943a, 93; Davies 1943b, pl. 122; van den Boorn 1988, 288.

[40] van den Boorn 1982, 379-80.

[41] Simpson 1965.

support this interpretation of the role of the vizier.[42] Furthermore, a stela found in Mersa Gawasis on the Red Sea coast reveals that Antefoker was involved in shipbuilding activities at Koptos.[43] He was ordered by his majesty to build ships to travel to Punt. It should however, be noted that whilst the Middle Kingdom vizier took on the role of overseeing important ventures such as journeys to Punt, the overall charge of *prw-nfr* was in the hands of the king's son Amenhotep.[44] Precisely what direct, if any, involvement the vizier had in shipbuilding during the New Kingdom remains unclear.

The role of the scribe

A number of scribes are known to be involved in the issuing of timbers to the *ḥmw.w wr* (chief/master craftsmen) in the Eighteenth Dynasty royal dockyard from P. BM 10056.[45] Further evidence of the scribal role comes from the Nineteenth Dynasty practice letter P. Anastasi IV, 7/9-8/7.[46] The letter was sent by Kageb, a *sš (n) pr-ḥd*, to the scribe Inena and the master craftsman (*ḥmw wr*) Amen-nakhte, and it gives them instructions for repairing a *skty*-bark and authorisation for the re-use of timber from another vessel.[47] The evidence suggests that the treasury was involved in the centralised activities of shipbuilding and repair through the supply or authorisation of the use of materials, the recording of labour and subsequent provision of rations.[48] It seems reasonable to assume that Aniy,[49] a *sš pr-ḥd n nb t3wy* 'Scribe of the treasury of the Lord of the Two Lands' as well as an *imy-r sšw mry(t) n nb t3wy* 'Overseer of records of the *mry(t)* of the Lord of the Two Lands' from the Ramesside Period, would have been involved in the overseeing of similar activities in his position of *imy-r*. The role of the Nineteenth Dynasty scribe of the dockyard, Amenemhat (*sš imn-m-ḥ3t n t3 wḫrt*)[50] was perhaps similar to that of Inena, who received the communications from the treasury and acted upon

them with the *ḥmw wr*. His role may have included the counting and issuing of timber as in P. BM 10056 or the accounting connected with the delivery of construction materials as in the 'Palace Accounts of Seti I'.[51]

The titles of the Eighteenth Dynasty official Nebamun[52] add to the understanding of the link between the dockyard and the treasury. He holds both scribal titles and titles pertaining to the role as overseer of the dockyard, *imy-r wḫrt*.[53] He holds three scribal titles; *sš*, *sš ḥsb ḥd nbw n nb t3wy* 'Scribe reckoning silver and gold of the Lord of the Two Lands' and *sš pr-ḥd n nswt m pr-nfr* 'Scribe of the treasury of the king in Perunefer'; as well as three titles referring to dockyards; *imy-r wḫrt n imn m niwt rsyt* 'Overseer of the dockyard of Amun in the southern city', *imy-r wḫrt imn-wsr-ḥ3t* 'Overseer of the dockyard of Amun-Userhat' and *imy-r wḫrt nswt* 'Overseer of the dockyard of the king' and the title of *imy-r pr* 'Overseer of the estate'.[54] His role as scribe of the treasury of the king in Perunefer provides a clear link between the royal dockyard and the treasury, which appears to be contemporary with the accounts of P. BM 10056.[55] His titles as *imy-r wḫrt* reveal that he was not only a scribe of the royal dockyard at Memphis, Perunefer, but also played a role in the

[42] Simpson 1960, 67, 70.

[43] Sayed 1977, 169-73; Sayed 1978, 70.

[44] Amenhotep is named in r. 16,1, v. 2,6 of the text: Glanville 1931, 106, 115, 117; Helck 1965, 277 (885). With regard to the reigning pharaoh at the time of the text, see Redford 1965.

[45] Glanville 1931, 120-1; Glanville 1932, 7-8.

[46] Caminos 1954, 159; Gardiner 1937, 42; Glanville 1932, 8; Helck 1965, 296 (904).

[47] In the Twelfth Dynasty, Wehemy, a *sš n pr-ḥd*, is mentioned in connection with the expenditure of work-days and the issuing of rations in the royal dockyard in P. Reisner II: Simpson 1965, 32, 41-2.

[48] Dürring 1995, 200.

[49] Gaballa 1975, 393.

[50] Amenemhat is known from the libation basin which he dedicated to Ptah, found in the Sanctuary of Rameses II at Mit Rahineh: Wall-Gordon 1958, 168.

[51] The Twelfth Dynasty text, P. Reisner II reveals that one of the functions of the scribe in the *wḫrt* would have been to count items of cargo being loaded and unloaded: Simpson 1965, 22-3. However, by the Ramesside Period the term mryt appears to be used in the context of a place of loading and unloading vessels. See for example the Amiens Papyrus: Gardiner 1948, 1-13; Gardiner 1941, 37-41; and the so-called 'Ship's Logs': Janssen 1961, passim. Thus the role of recording cargo may not have been one of Amenemhat's functions, but the overseeing of this activity may well have been one of Aniy's roles, who notably held titles in both the *mryt* and *pr-ḥd*.

[52] Nebamun (*Nb-imn*) is named as the owner of a Book of the Dead (P. BM 9964). The papyrus records his titles along with some of his family members as well as a number of the chapters of the Book of the Dead. Whilst the provenance of the papyrus is uncertain, its acquisition by Robert Hay who spent much of his time in Egypt on the Theban West Bank suggests a Theban provenance: Quirke 1993, 9, 46 no. 121. Munro 1988, 40-1, 290, suggested a date of Thutmose III to Amenhotep II for the papyrus and Bellion 1987, 53, stated the early Eighteenth Dynasty.

[53] The title *imy-r wḫrt* is attested from the Sixth Dynasty offering basin of Iy-Merer/Mery (Philadelphia E 13525) found in situ in G2098, a mastaba tomb at Giza: Fisher 1924, 63, pl. 48, no.3; Porter and Moss 1974, 99; cf. Dürring 1995, 180 C 23. The meaning of the title is again dependent upon the understanding of *wḫrt* in the Old Kingdom (see n. 11) as the context of the inscription provides no further evidence of any duties associated with the title.

[54] See Quirke 1993, 46 no. 121, 97, 102, 103, 104 for titles and translations, but cf. Eichler 2000, 287 no. 312; Luft 1977, 71; Munro 1988, 290; Naville 1886, 58; Taylor 2001, nos. 150-2, no. 2050.

[55] See note 52 for suggested dates of the papyrus.

administration of a royal dockyard(s) in Thebes. It remains uncertain, however, whether these titles were held sequentially or simultaneously.

ḥmw wr, ḥmw.w and mḏḥ.w

Whilst P. BM 10056 provides an insight into the organisation and administration of a royal dockyard of the Eighteenth Dynasty, there are nonetheless limits to the information it provides. Eyre argued that the issues of timber in P. BM 10056 were rather small and irregular: no pattern of days worked can be worked out, and there is no indication of whether the ḥmw.w wr worked alone or if they supervised work crews (ḥmw.w and mḏḥ.w).[56] With regard to this latter issue it is clear that the title ḥmw wr was of higher rank than the ḥmw.w and the mḏḥ.w.[57] The Eighteenth Dynasty stela of Iuna (BM 1332) reveals that he was the overseer of the boatbuilders, mḏḥ, in the description: ḥmw wr n mḏḥ wỉꜣw n nṯrw nb(w) šmꜥw tꜣ-mḥw.[58] This would suggest that the ḥmw.w wr did have work crews for the construction of divine vessels presumably within a state dockyard of unknown location. The relationship of the ḥmw wr as the superior of the ḥmw.w can be seen at the end of the New Kingdom in a model letter in P. Lansing.[59] There is, however, no clear evidence of the relationship between the mḏḥ.w and the ḥmw.w.[60]

Conclusion

There are limitations to the evidence regarding the social structure of those places involved in shipbuilding and repair. However, there are a number of cases of titles that had been associated with such activities in the Old and Middle Kingdoms but which are no longer attested in the New Kingdom. There are even instances, such as the pry, where the role of the individuals holding the title appears to have changed. The titles reveal changing social structures over time and possibly space. It therefore seems more appropriate to view any social structure within a tighter chronological framework so as not to hide those very changes in the organisation of vessel construction and repair. Interpreting them within long periods such as the New Kingdom, when a great deal

of social, political and religious change took place, risks missing the subtleties of the organisation of these social environments.

Acknowledgements

I would like to thank Prof. W. J. Tait of the Institute of Archaeology, University College London, for valuable comments on the paper.

Angus Graham
Institute of Archaeology
University College London

Cited works

Arnold, D.
1991 *Building in Egypt: Pharaonic Stone Masonry*. New York and Oxford: Oxford University Press.

Bellion, M.
1987 *Égypte ancienne. Catalogue des manuscrits hiéroglyphiques et hiératiques et des dessins, sur papyrus, cuir ou tissu, publiés ou signals*. Pau: Madeleine Bellion.

Blackman, A. M. and M. R. Apted
1953 *The Rock Tombs of Meir V: The Tomb-Chapels A, No. 1 (that of Ni-'Ankh-Pepi the Black), A, No.2 (that of Pepi'Onkh with the 'Good Name' of Heny the Black), A, No. 4 (that of Hepi the Black), D, No.4 (that of Pepi), and E, Nos. 1-4 (those of Meniu, Nenki, Pepi'Onkh and Tjetu)*. London: EES; Archaeological Survey of Egypt 28.

van den Boorn, G. P. F.
1982 'On the Date of "The Duties of the Vizier"', *Orientalia* 51: 369-81.
1988 *The Duties of the Vizier. Civil Administration in the Early New Kingdom*. London: Kegan Paul International; Studies in Egyptology.

de Buck, A.
1954 *The Egyptian Coffin Texts V: Texts of Spells 355-471*. Chicago: The University of Chicago Press; The University of Chicago Oriental Institute Publications 73.

Caminos, R. A.
1954 *Late-Egyptian Miscellanies*. London: Oxford University Press; Brown Egyptological Studies 1.

Darnell, D. and J. Darnell
1997 'Exploring the "Narrow Doors" of the Theban Desert', *Egyptian Archaeology* 10: 24-6.

Davies, N. de G.
1902 *The Rock Tombs of Deir el Gebrâwi I: Tomb of Aba and Smaller Tombs of the Southern Group*. London: EEF; Archaeological Survey of Egypt 11.
1943a *The Tomb of Rekh-mi-Re at Thebes* I. New York: Plantin; The Metropolitan Museum of Art Egyptian Expedition 11.

---

[56] Eyre 1987b, 196.
[57] Steinmann 1982, 66-9; Steinmann 1980, 141.
[58] For the stela of Iuna (ỉwnꜣ) with the list of all the divine barks for which he was the chief craftsman, see Edwards 1939, 38-40, pl. 33; Glanville 1932, 39-40. With regard to the date, Glanville 1932, 39 suggested a date of mid to late Eighteenth Dynasty and Helck 1971, 356 proposed the reign of Thutmose IV.
[59] P. Lansing 5/2-4, Caminos 1954, 384-5; Gardiner 1937, 103-4.
[60] A single example of the title ḥmw-mḏḥ is known, but it is unclear what its significance might be: Steinmann 1980, 151.

1943b *The Tomb of Rekh-mi-Re at Thebes* II. New York: Plantin; The Metropolitan Museum of Art Egyptian Expedition 11.

Drenkhahn, R.
1976 *Die Handwerker und ihre Tätigkeiten im alten Ägypten*. Wiesbaden: Harrassowitz; Ägyptologische Abhandlungen 31.
1995 'Artisans and Artists in Pharaonic Egypt', in J. M. Sasson, J. Baines, G. Beckman and K. S. Rubinson (eds) *Civilizations of the Ancient Near East* I. New York: Simon & Schuster Macmillan, 331-43.

Duell, P.
1938 *The Mastaba of Mereruka* II: *Chambers A 11-13. Doorjambs and Inscriptions of Chambers A 1-21. Tomb Chamber Exterior. Plates 104-219*. Chicago: The University of Chicago Press; The University of Chicago Oriental Institute Publications 39.

Dürring, N.
1995 *Materialien zum Schiffbau im alten Ägypten*. Berlin: Achet-Verlag; Abhandlungen des Deutschen Archäologischen Instituts Kairo Ägyptologische Reihe 11.

Edwards, I. E. S. (ed.)
1939 *British Museum Hieroglyphic Texts from Egyptian Stelae etc.* VIII. London: The British Museum.

Eichler, S. S.
2000 *Die Verwaltung des "Hauses des Amun" in der 18. Dynastie*. Hamburg: Helmut Buske Verlag; Studien zur Altägyptischen Kultur, Beihefte 7.

Erman, A. and H. O. Lange
1925 *Papyrus Lansing: Eine ägyptische Schulhandschrift der 20. Dynastie*. Copenhagen: A. F. Høst & Søn; Copenhagen. Kgl. Danske Videnskabernes Selskab. Historisk-filologiske Meddeleser, 10, 3.

Eyre, C. J.
1987a 'Work and the Organisation of Work in the Old Kingdom', in M. A. Powell (ed.), *Labor in the Ancient Near East*. New Haven: American Oriental Society; American Oriental Series 68, 5-47.
1987b 'Work and the Organisation of Work in the New Kingdom', in M. A. Powell (ed.), *Labor in the Ancient Near East*. New Haven: American Oriental Society; American Oriental Series 68, 167-221.

Faulkner, R. O.
1962 *A Concise Dictionary of Middle Egyptian*. Oxford: Griffith Institute.
1977 *The Ancient Egyptian Coffin Texts* II: *Spells 355-787*. Warminster: Aris and Phillips Ltd.

Fisher, C. S.
1924 *The Minor Cemetery at Giza*. Philadelphia: University Museum; University of Pennsylvania, Egyptian Section of the University Museum: The Eckley B. Coxe Jr. Foundation New Series 1.

Gaballa, G. A.
1975 'The Chief of Records of the Royal Harbour Aniy (Amenemone)', *Orientalia* 44: 388-94.

Gardiner, A. H.
1937 *Late-Egyptian Miscellanies*. Brussels: Fondation égyptologique reine Élisabeth; Bibliotheca Aegyptiaca 7.
1941 'Ramesside Texts relating to the Taxation and Transport of Corn', *JEA* 27: 19-73.
1947 *Ancient Egyptian Onomastica* I: *Text*. London: Oxford University Press.
1948 *Ramesside Administrative Documents*. London: Oxford University Press; Published on behalf of the Griffith Institute, Ashmolean Museum, Oxford.

Glanville, S. R. K.
1931 'Records of a Royal Dockyard of the Time of Tuthmosis III: Papyrus British Museum 10056', *ZÄS* 66: 105-21.
1932 'Records of a Royal Dockyard of the Time of Tuthmosis III: Papyrus British Museum 10056 (Part II)', *ZÄS* 68: 7-41.

Grandet, P.
1994 *Le Papyrus Harris I (BM 9999)* II. Le Caire: Institut français d'archéologie orientale; Bibliothèque d'étude 109/2.

Haring, B. J. J.
1997 *Divine Households. Administrative and Economic Aspects of the New Kingdom Royal Memorial Temples in Western Thebes*. Leiden: Nederlands Instituut voor het Nabije Oosten; Egyptologische Uitgaven 12.

Hassan, F. A.
1993 'Town and Village in Ancient Egypt: Ecology, Society and Urbanization', in T. Shaw, P. Sinclair, B. Andah and A. Okpoko (eds), *The Archaeology of Africa: Food, Metal and Towns*. London: Routledge, 551-69.
1997 'The Dynamics of a Riverine Civilization: A Geoarchaeological Perspective on the Nile Valley, Egypt', *World Archaeology* 29(1): 51-74.

Helck, W.
1965 *Materialien zur Wirtschaftsgeschichte des Neuen Reiches (Teil V)* III: *Eigentum und Besitz an verschiedenen Dingen des täglichen Lebens. Kapitel AI – AL.* Wiesbaden: Verlag der Akademie der Wissenschaften und der Literatur in Mainz, in Kommission bei Franz Steiner; Akademie der Wissenschaften und der Literatur. Geistes- und Sozialwissenschaftlichen Klasse, Abhandlungen 1964, 4.
1971 *Die Beziehungen Ägyptens zu Vorderasien im 3. und 2. Jahrtausend v. Chr.*, 2. verbesserte Auflage. Wiesbaden: Otto Harrassowitz; Ägyptologische Abhandlungen 5.

Hornell, J.
1943 'On the Carrying Capacity of Ramesside Grain-ships', *JEA* 29: 76-8.

Janssen, J. J.
1961 *Two Ancient Egyptian Ship's Logs: Papyrus Leiden 1 350 verso and Papyrus Turin 2008 + 2016.* Leiden: E. J. Brill; Oudheidkundige Mededelingen uit het Rijksmuseum van Oudheden te Leiden: Supplement op Nieuwe Reeks 52.

Jeffreys, D. G.
1996 'House, Palace and Islands at Memphis', in M. Bietak (ed.), *Haus und Palast im Alten Ägypten.* Vienna: Verlag Der Österreichischen Akademie Der Wissenschaften; Untersuchungen der Zweigstelle Kairo des Österreichischen Archäologischen Institutes 14, 287-94.

Jones, D.
1988 *A Glossary of Ancient Egyptian Nautical Titles and Terms.* London: Kegan Paul International.
2000 *An Index of Ancient Egyptian Titles, Epithets and Phrases of the Old Kingdom.* 2 volumes. Oxford: BAR Publishing; BAR International Series 866.

Kamish, M.
1986 'Problems of Toponymy with Special Reference to Memphis and *PRW-NFR*', *Wepwawet* 3: 32-6.

Kemp, B. and D. O'Connor
1974 'An Ancient Nile Harbour: University Museum Excavations at the 'Birket Habu'', *International Journal of Nautical Archaeology and Underwater Exploration* 3/1, 101-36.

Kitchen, K. A.
1993a *Ramesside Inscriptions. Translated and Annotated: Translations* I: *Ramesses I, Sethos I and Contemporaries.* Oxford: Blackwell Reference.
1993b *Ramesside Inscriptions. Translated and Annotated: Notes and Comments* I: *Ramesses I, Sethos I and Contemporaries.* Oxford: Blackwell Reference.
1975 *Ramesside Inscriptions: Historical and Biographical* I. Oxford: Blackwell.

Lesko, L. H. and B. S. Lesko
1982 *A Dictionary of Late Egyptian* I. Berkeley: B.C. Scribe Publications.

Luft, U.
1977 'Das Totenbuch des Ptahmose. Papyrus Kraków MNK IX - 752/1-4', *ZÄS* 104: 46-75.

Moussa, A. M. and H. Altenmüller
1977 *Das Grab des Nianchchnum und Chnumhotep.* Mainz am Rhein: Philipp von Zabern; Old Kingdom Tombs at the Causeway of King Unas at Saqqara. Deutsches Archäologisches Instituts Abteilung Kairo, Archäologische Veröffentlichungen 21.

Munro, I.
1988 *Untersuchungen zu den Totenbuch-Papyri der 18. Dynastie. Kriterien ihrer Datierung. D 7 "Göttinger Philosophische Dissertation"* (Studies on the Book of Dead of the 18th Dynasty). London and New York: Kegan Paul International; Studies in Egyptology.

Naville, É.
1886 *Das ägyptische Todtenbuch der XVIII. bis XX. Dynastie. Einleitung.* Berlin: A. Asher & Co.

Newberry, P. E.
1893 *Beni Hasan* I. London: EES; Archaeological Survey of Egypt 1.

Porter, B. and R. L. B. Moss
1934 *Topographical Bibliography of Ancient Egyptian Hieroglyphic Texts, Reliefs and Paintings* IV: *Lower and Middle Egypt. (Delta and Cairo to Asyût).* Oxford: Clarendon Press.
1974 *Topographical Bibliography of Ancient Egyptian Hieroglyphic Texts, Reliefs and Paintings* III: *Memphis. Part 1: Abû Rawâsh to Abûsîr.* Second edition revised and augmented by J Málek. Oxford: Griffith Institute, Ashmolean Museum.

Petrie, W. M. F.
1892 *Medum.* London: David Nutt.

Quirke, S. G. J.
1993 *Owners of Funerary Papyri in the British Museum.* London: Department of Egyptian Antiquities, British Museum; Occasional Paper 92.

Redford, D. B.
1965 'The Coregency of Tuthmosis III and Amenophis II', *JEA* 51: 107-22.

Save-Söderbergh, T.
1946 *The Navy of the Eighteenth Egyptian Dynasty.* Uppsala: A.-B. Lundequistska Bokhandeln; Uppsala Universitets Årsskrift 1946: 6.

Sayed, A. M. A. H.
1977 'Discovery of the 12th Dynasty Port at Wadi Gawasis on the Red Sea Shore', *RdE* 29: 138-78.
1978 'The Recently Discovered Port on the Red Sea Shore', *JEA* 64: 69-71.

Simpson, W. K.
1960 'Papyrus Lythgoe: A Fragment of a Literary Text of the Middle Kingdom from el-Lisht', *JEA* 46: 65-70.
1965 *Accounts of the Dockyard Workshop at This in the Reign of Sesostris I. Papyrus Reisner* II: *Transcription and Commentary.* Boston: Museum of Fine Arts.

Spiegelberg, W. (ed.)
1904 *Ägyptische Grabsteine und Denksteine aus süddeutschen Sammlungen* II: *München.* Strassburg i. E.: Schlesier & Schweikhardt.

Steindorff, G.
1913 *Das Grab des Ti.* Leipzig: J. C. Hinrichs; Veröffentlichungen der Ernst von Sieglin Expedition in Ägypten 2.

Steinmann, F.

1980 'Untersuchungen zu den in der handwerklich-künstlerischen Produktion beschäftigten Personen und Berufsgruppen des Neuen Reiches', *ZÄS* 107: 137-57.

1982 'Untersuchungen zu den in der handwerklich-künstlerischen Produktion beschäftigten Personen und Berufsgruppen des Neuen Reichs II: Klassifizierung der Berufsbezeichnungen und Titel', *ZÄS* 109: 66-72.

1991 'Untersuchungen zu den in der handwerklich-künstlerischen Produktion beschäftigten Personen und Berufsgruppen des Neuen Reiches V. Bemerkungen zur sozialen Stellung und materiellen Lage', *ZÄS* 118: 149-61.

Taylor, J. A.

2001 *An Index of Male Non-Royal Egyptian Titles, Epithets & Phrases of the 18th Dynasty*. London: Museum Bookshop Publications.

Vandorpe, K.

1995 '"The Dockyard Workshop" or the Toachris Village', *Enchoria* 22: 158-68.

Wall-Gordon, H.

1958 'A New Kingdom Libation Basin Dedicated to Ptah, Second Part: The Inscriptions', *MDAIK* 16: 168-75.

Wild, H.

1953 *Le Tombeau de Ti* II: *La Chapelle (Première Partie)*. Le Caire: Institut français d'archéologie orientale; Mémoires publiés par les membres de l'institut français d'archéologie orientale du Caire, sous la direction de M. Ch. Kuentz 65.

Wreszinski, W.

1923 *Atlas zur altägyptischen Kulturgeschichte* I *fasc.* II *(151-424)*. Leipzig: J. C. Hinrichs.

Zayed, A. el H.

1987 'Perou – Nefer: Port de Guerre d'Amenophis II', *ASAE* 66: 75-109.

Egyptian Blue: Where, When, How?

Gareth D. Hatton, A. J. Shortland and M. S. Tite

Introduction

Vitreous materials are defined as those materials that contain significant amounts of glass, either as a surface glaze or more widely dispersed throughout their structure. The earliest type of vitreous material to appear in the archaeological record in Egypt was glazed stone, followed later by faience and Egyptian blue and culminating in the high-tech large-scale production of various coloured glasses. The technologies for the production of these materials are likely to be closely related, since they are all silicate technologies and utilise the same range of raw materials. This paper deals solely with the introduction and use of Egyptian blue.

Definition

Egyptian blue was the first synthetic pigment to be produced in antiquity. The date of the first use of Egyptian blue is thought by most authors to be the Fourth Dynasty in Egypt,[1] though some authors[2] have suggested that it may have first been developed in Mesopotamia during the same period. It continued in use through to the Roman Period and was distributed throughout the Roman Empire in the form of pigments and mosaic tesserae with finds known as far afield as England, France, Malta and Italy.[3] In Egypt it was the most common blue pigment during Dynastic times[4] and is found on many tombs and temples even today.

The pigment Egyptian blue is a polycrystalline glass composite. It consists of three main phases: quartz, the Egyptian blue mineral (a copper calcium tetrasilicate of the formula $CuCaSi_4O_{10}$, sometimes written $CuO.CaO.4SiO_2$) and a glass matrix. Since the Egyptian blue mineral has a set composition (known as its stoichiometry), any variation in the bulk composition of Egyptian blue pigments will be due either to the varying proportion of quartz in the material, or to a variance in the composition or relative proportion of the glass. Table 1 illustrates some of the analyses that have been undertaken to find the overall composition of Egyptian blue from various sites and how these are different from the ideal composition of the Egyptian blue mineral. The individual phases present within a sample of Egyptian blue can be distinguished in the SEM by their back-scatter contrast, the relic quartz grains being the darkest grey, the glass phase a mid-grey and the Egyptian blue mineral a light grey (see Figure 1). Any copper present as discrete particles will show as white.

Within the literature the terminology for Egyptian blue is confused with many different terms used for this material, among the most common being blue paste (which can lead to confusion with faience) and blue frit. Within this paper the term Egyptian blue is used solely to describe this composite material and not the copper calcium tetrasilicate phase, which will be described as the 'Egyptian blue mineral'. This mineral phase has a naturally occurring analogue, cuprorivaite, but this is very rare and is not thought to have been used in antiquity. Egyptian blue is therefore an entirely synthetic, man-made compound.

There is little direct evidence for the production of Egyptian blue during ancient times, and little mention of it in contemporary texts. An exception to this is Vitruvius who, in his *Ten Books on Architecture*, includes a method of 'making blue'. This is interpreted to be the manufacture of Egyptian blue.[5] In his account Vitruvius described a method of production thus 'Sand and the flowers of natron are brayed together so finely that the product is like meal, and copper is grated...over to form a conglomerate'.[6] Further information is included in the text as to the actual manufacture of the pigment in balls 'it is made into balls by rolling it in the hands...The dry balls are put in an earthen jar, and the jars in an oven'.[7] The suggestion in the text is that the production was large-scale with many 'jars' being fired at once, and importantly there is contemporary archaeological evidence to support this at Memphis, Egypt. Here large Nile silt vessels were found during excavations by Petrie, which contained large numbers of balls composed of Egyptian blue approximately two centimetres in diameter.[8]

---

[1] Lucas and Harris 1962, 342.
[2] Ullrich 1987, 326; shells containing pigment have been found at Kish.
[3] Tite et al. 1984, 239.
[4] Lucas and Harris, 1962, 340; El Goresy et al. 1986.

[5] Morgan 1960, 218-19.
[6] ibid. 218.
[7] ibid. 218-19.
[8] Such as UC47305, Petrie Museum, UCL.

Uses and occurrences of Egyptian blue

Table 2 charts some of the known uses and occurrences of Egyptian blue in Egypt and elsewhere to give an impression of the widespread nature of the pigment. It also highlights that Egyptian blue was distributed throughout the Roman Empire and was long lived in its use. As the table shows, there is an early occurrence in a wall painting during the Fourth Dynasty and the first objects, in early cases cylinder seals and scarabs, seem to appear from the Sixth Dynasty onwards. However, finds of the pigment are distributed far and wide. In one study[9] on the distribution of colours in wall paintings, more than fifty tombs were studied, including archaeological sites in Egypt which were from the Fifth, Sixth, Eleventh, Twelfth, and Eighteenth to Twentieth Dynasties. They found that in all but a few examples Egyptian blue was the only blue pigment used. Further research has continued to demonstrate that Egyptian blue was the predominant blue pigment, with less robust pigments such as azurite occasionally being applied.[10]

Egyptian blue has been found as the blue pigment in many wall paintings of the Late Bronze Age (see Table 2) in the Greek islands, suggesting either that Egyptian blue from Egypt was being imported into Greece or that it was being manufactured locally. During the Roman Empire the use of Egyptian blue as a blue pigment was common with examples known throughout the Mediterranean and Europe. Isolated finds have also been found as far north as Scotland[11] and Norway.[12] However, after the Roman Period there is scant evidence for its use.[13] The rapid decline of the use of the pigment in post Roman contexts could be attributed to a number of factors. The introduction of an alternative blue pigment, possibly ultramarine (natural, composed of ground lapis lazuli, later artificially produced) or smalt, basically a ground cobalt coloured glass, could account for its disuse.[14] Natron used in the production of Egyptian blue may not have been available after the fall of the Roman Empire, which may account for this decline.[15] The fall of the Roman Empire may also have resulted in a drop in demand for the pigment leading eventually to its demise. The occasional occurrences in Post-Roman contexts, for example the use of Egyptian blue in a

ninth century fresco in Rome[16] may therefore be due to the reutilization of earlier Roman pieces.

Historiography

Egyptian blue has been subjected to many and varied studies, concentrating on characterising its attributes, the evolution of the technology associated with its manufacture and its place in the greater scheme of Egyptian, and indeed technological, development. So many are there that it would be unwise to undertake in this short paper any evaluation of all the works describing Egyptian blue. However, a few seminal works must be highlighted. The first analysis of Egyptian blue began with Davy's *Some Experiments and Observation on the Colours Used in Painting by the Ancients*[17] where the pigment found in a pot during excavation at Pompeii was analysed by wet chemistry. This analysis provided the first idea of how the composition of this striking blue compound was obtained. The development of less destructive techniques led to a greater number of samples being examined by a number of authors, many of whom are noteworthy here. The most comprehensive study undertaken to date consists of approximately fifty samples from Egyptian and Mesopotamian contexts along with Roman samples within Europe and the Mediterranean.[18] Other papers of note are the comprehensive study of wall painting within Egypt undertaken by El Goresy et al., already discussed,[19] where the change in the raw materials used to produce Egyptian blue through time was suggested. It was proposed that the copper bearing raw material was originally malachite or pure copper, but this changed to a bronze on the basis of tin being present within the later samples studied. The most recent analyses have concentrated on single samples and the variability within them,[20] along with the characterisation of the pigment by other analytical methods.[21]

Much work has been done on the experimental replication of Egyptian blue. A number of authors have successfully prepared it from a mixture of malachite, calcium carbonate, silica and a sodium carbonate flux heated together at under 1050°C. The reaction undertaken at this temperature is as follows

[9] El Goresy et al. 1986.

[10] See Lucas and Harris 1962, 340.

[11] Campbell 1991, 162.

[12] Riederer 1997, 41.

[13] For example two wall paintings from the ninth century AD (see Table 2).

[14] See Orna et al. 1980 for discussion on the introduction of synthetic blue pigments.

[15] This may also be applied to glass production.

[16] Lazzarini 1982; This painting is in the lower church of San Clemente.

[17] Davy 1815.

[18] Tite et al. 1984.

[19] El Goresy et al. 1986; Jaksch et al. 1983.

[20] Delamare 1998.

[21] See Mirti et al. 1995; Bruni et al. 1999.

$Cu_2CO_3(OH)_2$
$+8SiO_2+2CaCO_3 \rightarrow 2CaCuSi_4O_{10}+3CO_2+H_2O$

This replication work began with Laurie,[22] but more recently Ullrich,[23] Tite et al.[24] and Delamare[25] have contributed. While the experimental reproduction of Egyptian blue has been successful, there is much debate over the detail and only a few general points are widely agreed. Egyptian blue can be obtained by mixing raw materials with flux and heating to a temperature of 850-1000°C, although the exact temperature to form the highest quality pigment is unknown. The highest temperature of the production of the pigment is set at 1050°C as the pigment decomposes at this temperature in an oxidising atmosphere.[26] In addition, flux quantity and the form of copper is still controversial[27] but this is considered to vary over time.[28] Laurie et al. suggested from the results of their experimentation that the production of Egyptian blue was a multi-stage process and that the primary product was powdered and fired more than once.[29] This production in two stages is likely[30] though it is unnecessary to introduce the idea of multiple firings to produce coarse Egyptian blue.[31] Specific production strategies may be employed for the production of specific qualities of pigment dependent upon their intended use. To this end further processing of the 'raw' single fired pigment may be undertaken. The production of objects may again be a separate processing of the primary or 'raw' pigment. This would fit with the idea that accurate control of the reaction is needed for the production of the high quality blue pigment as other phases may form if the mix is not right.[32]

Technological questions

How Egyptian blue was first discovered is a problematic question, which must be investigated with reference to the production of other early silicate technologies. Certainly, some authors have attributed the discovery of glass, one of the last of the silicate technologies to be discovered, to developments in the faience technology.[33] There is also a potential link between Egyptian blue and faience, especially the blue-green faience from the Predynastic and Early Dynastic Periods, and this can be illustrated by the similarity in their calcium copper ratio.[34] The fact that both Egyptian blue and faience have a weight percent CaO:CuO ratio of approximately 0.7 is striking. Only the high flux content and presence of the pure silica core in faience prevents the formation of the Egyptian blue mineral. Egyptian blue may therefore have been discovered during faience making when different quantities of the faience glazing formula was added to the sand rather than applied to the siliceous body.[35]

Egyptian blue was used not only as a pigment but also as a material out of which objects could be formed. The question is, when did this occur? It has been suggested that the production of glass led to the addition of glass to the pigment Egyptian blue, giving it enough cohesion for the objects and to support its own weight.[36] This introduction of glass to the mixture would lead to a clear change in microstructure and a difference between Egyptian blue made into an object and that of the raw pigment or pigment cakes. However, this is not the case as small objects predate glass significantly. For example, scaraboids of Egyptian blue are well attested from the Twelfth Dynasty[37] and cylinder seals from as early as the Sixth Dynasty.[38] Technologically, Egyptian blue continued throughout its history with very little change to its overall composition. While there are observable differences in colour, as can be seen by Russell's[39] description of the pigments found at Medum, this variation can occur within a single site and so can be discounted as a function of time or change in technological tradition.

Conclusion

As can be seen from this paper there are many unknowns still remaining. Some of these questions relate to trade - as we have seen in this paper the pigment has been discovered in many different contexts, but how did it get there? Was it a locally manufactured pigment or were there many workshops all producing Egyptian blue? Others relate to technology - were there distinct workshops? Was there a single recipe to work to or was it more haphazard? Yet more relate to the discovery of the pigment. The background of its discovery may also

[22] Laurie et al. 1914.
[23] Ullrich 1987.
[24] Tite et al. 1984.
[25] Delamare 1998.
[26] See Mirti et al. 1995.
[27] ibid.
[28] See El Goresy 1986.
[29] Laurie et al. 1914, 423.
[30] Tite et al. 1984; El Goresy 1986, 15.
[31] Tite et al. 1987.
[32] Mirti et al. 1995.
[33] See Nicholson 1995.

[34] See Kaczmarczyk and Hedges 1983, 152.
[35] Laurie et al. 1914, 428.
[36] Chase 1968, 88.
[37] See Petrie 1917.
[38] See Hall 1913 (BM 47460 and 29061).
[39] Russell 1892.

answer the question of whether the pigment should be more accurately called 'Near Eastern blue' rather than Egyptian blue. Further work will be undertaken to address these questions.

Gareth D. Hatton
A. J. Shortland
M. S. Tite

Research Laboratory of Archaeology and the History of Art
Oxford University

Table 1: Crystal stoichiometry and various bulk chemical analyses from other studies

	SiO$_2$	CuO	CaO	Na$_2$O
Crystal Stoichiometry	63.9	21.2	14.9	---
Brill 1999				
Egypt	67.4	12.7	14.4	1.2
Mesopotamia	73.3	12	8.9	0.8
Other	75.5	10.6	8.5	0.9
Delamare 1998	57	21.2	16.4	1.5
Jaksch et al. 1983	60.7	11.7	20.2	2.5
Tite et al. 1984				
Egypt	65.4	14.7	11.9	1.4
Mesopotamia	64.2	17.6	10.8	0.3
Other	66.3	13.6	11.5	1.6

Table 2: Some occurrences of Egyptian blue

Location	Date	Paper	Further Information
Egypt	4th Dynasty	Ullrich 1987	Pyramid Texts
Saqqara, Egypt	5th Dynasty (one 6th)	Jaksch et al.1983	Six occurrences
Egypt	6th Dynasty	Hall 1913	Two cylinder seals
El Khoka, Egypt	6th Dynasty	Jaksch et al.1983	
Gizeh, Egypt	6th Dynasty	Jaksch et al.1983	
Asswan, Egypt	6th Dynasty	Jaksch et al.1983	
Thebes, Egypt	11th Dynasty	Jaksch et al.1983	
Beni Hassan, Egypt	11th Dynasty	Jaksch et al.1983	Two samples
Egypt	11th Dynasty	Laurie et al. 1914	Coffin lid
Asswan	12th Dynasty	Jaksch et al.1983	Two samples
Thebes, Egypt	12th Dynasty	Jaksch et al.1983	
Beni Hassan, Egypt	12th Dynasty	Jaksch et al.1983	Two samples
El Kab, Egypt	18th Dynasty	Jaksch et al.1983	Contains tin
Luxor, Egypt	18th Dynasty	Jaksch et al.1983	Three samples (all contain tin)
Thebes, Egypt	18th Dynasty	Jaksch et al.1983	Sixteen samples (Twelve with tin present)
Amarna South, Egypt	18th Dynasty	Jaksch et al.1983	Four samples (three contain tin)
Amarna North, Egypt	18th Dynasty	Jaksch et al.1983	Four samples (one contains tin)
Egypt	18th Dynasty	Laurie et al. 1914	
Amarna, Egypt	18th Dynasty	Brill 1999	Eight samples (three with tin over 1%)
Egypt		Brill 1999	Three samples (one with tin over 1%)
Palace of Amenhotep III, Egypt	18th Dynasty	Brill 1999	Three samples (all with tin over 0.9%)
Amarna, Egypt	18th Dynasty	Tite 1994	Fifteen samples
Amarna, Egypt	18th Dynasty	Tite et al. 1984	Eight samples (One with significant tin)
Thebes, Egypt	New Kingdom	Tite 1987	Four samples
Egypt	c.1350 BC	Tite et al. 1980	Slab of pigment
Egypt	c.1350 BC	Tite et al. 1980	Disc cover fragment
Deir el Medina, Egypt	19th Dynasty	Jaksch et al.1983	Contains tin
Abydos, Egypt	19th Dynasty	Jaksch et al.1983	Contains tin
Kanais, Egypt	19th Dynasty	Jaksch et al.1983	Contains tin
Thebes, Egypt	19th Dynasty	Jaksch et al.1983	Five samples (all contain tin)

Beth el-Wali, Egypt	19th Dynasty	Jaksch et al.1983	Contains tin
Thebes, Egypt	20th Dynasty	Jaksch et al.1983	Contains tin
Knossos, Greece	18th-17th Century BC	Profi et al. 1976	Three on plaster (contains tin)
Thera, Santorini	17th-16th Century BC	Profi et al. 1977	Five on plaster (contains tin)
Iraq	15th-13th Century BC	Pollard and Moorey 1982	Two tubular beads (0.1% tin)
Nuzi	15th Century BC	Brill 1999	Four samples
Mycenae	15th-11th Century BC	Profi et al. 1974	Seven on plaster, three raw pigments (contains tin)
Tiryns	14th Century BC	Riederer 1997	
Mycenae	13th Century BC	Brill 1999	Two samples
Hasanlu	11th-9th Century BC	Brill 1999	Three samples
Nineveh	9th-7th Century BC	Tite et al. 1987	
Nineveh	9th-7th Century BC	Tite et al. 1984	Nine samples (one with 0.9% tin)
Nimrud	9th-7th Century BC	Tite et al. 1987	
Nimrud	9th-7th Century BC	Tite et al. 1984	Ten samples
Nimrud	7th Century BC	Brill 1999	Seven samples
Mesopotamia	800-400 BC	Tite et al. 1980	Block
Egypt	600 BC	Tite et al. 1987	Fragment
Egypt	c.600 BC	Tite et al. 1980	Figure
Aegina, Greece	580-500 BC	Riederer 1997	
Tell el Yahudja, Egypt	6th-5th Century BC	Tite et al. 1984	0.9% tin
Persepolis	6th Century BC	Brill 1999	Two samples
Persepolis and Pasagadae	6th-4th Century BC	Stodulski et al. 1984	12 Samples
Pella, Greece	400-108 BC	Riederer 1997	
Petosiris, Egypt	333 BC	Jaksch et al.1983	Contains tin
Luxor Karnak, Egypt	320 BC	Jaksch et al.1983	Contains tin
Egypt	300 BC	Tite et al. 1984	Eight samples (five with significant tin)
Egypt	300 BC	Tite et al. 1987	Fragment
Asswan, Egypt	Ptolemaic Roman	Jaksch et al.1983	Two samples (both contain tin)
Komombo, Egypt	Ptolemaic Roman	Jaksch et al.1983	
Vergina, Greece	4th Century BC	Filippakis et al. 1979	Three pigments (contains tin, lead and zinc)
Rhodes	Hellenistic	Brill 1999	
Münsingen, Switzerland	2nd Century BC	Riederer 1997	
Pompeii	1st Century BC	Riederer 1997	
Lyon, France	1st Century AD	Ullrich 1987	Ball
Dormus Aygustana, Palatine	1st Century AD	Tite et al. 1984	
Sollas, North Uist, UK	1st-2nd Century AD	Campbell 1991	Dark blue piece 1 cm
Harian's Villa, Tivoli	2nd Century AD	Tite et al. 1984	
Harian's Villa, Piazzadoro	2nd Century AD	Tite et al. 1984	
Italy	2nd Century AD	Tite et al. 1987	Tessera
Malta	2nd Century AD	Tite et al. 1984	
Hölstein, Switzerland	2nd Century AD	Riederer 1997	
Cologne, Germany	2nd-3rd Century AD	Riederer 1997	
Springhead, Kent, UK	2nd-3rd Century AD	Brill 1999	
Malta	3rd Century AD	Tite et al. 1987	Pigment ball
Akhmim, Egypt	3rd-4th Century AD	Sack et al. 1981	Painted canvas
Bø, Norway	350 AD	Riederer 1997	
Egypt	Roman	Hillyer 1984	Five mummy cloths painted (contains tin)
Aosta, Italy	Roman	Mirti et al. 1995	
Sicily	Roman	Brill 1999	
Memphis	Roman	Brill 1999	
Spain	Roman	Brill 1999	
Palatine Hill	Roman	Laurie et al. 1914	Fresco
Viriconium, UK	Roman	Laurie et al. 1914	Two samples

Marseilles, France	Roman	Tite et al. 1984	
Braughing, Herts, UK	Romano-British	Tite et al. 1984	
Berkhampstead, UK	Romano-British	Tite et al. 1984	
Water Newton, UK	Romano-British	Biek 1982 Table I	Pellets
Chichester, UK	Romano-British	Biek 1982 Table I	Pot with fine pigment
Rudston, UK	Romano-British	Biek 1982 Table I	Pellet
Hayton, UK	Romano-British	Biek 1982 Table I	Potsherd with powder
Tower of London, UK	Romano-British	Biek 1982 Table I	Pellets and lump
Colchester, UK	Romano-British	Biek 1982 Table I	Pellets
Richborogh, UK	Romano-British	Biek 1982 Table I	Lump (12x8x5 cm)
Catsgore, UK	Romano-British	Biek 1982 Table I	Lump
Downton, UK	Romano-British	Biek 1982 Table II	Painted plaster
Verulamium, UK	Romano-British	Biek 1982 Table II	Painted plaster
Stanton Low, UK	Romano-British	Biek 1982 Table II	Painted plaster
Darenth, UK	Romano-British	Biek 1982 Table II	Painted plaster
Woodeaton, UK	Romano-British	Biek 1982 Table II	Palette and pellet
Silchester, UK	Romano-British	Biek 1982 Table II	Pellet
Wroxeter, UK	Romano-British	Biek 1982 Table II	Pellet
York, UK	Romano-British	Biek 1982 Table II	Painted plaster
San Clemente, Rome	9th Century AD	Lazzarini 1982	Wall painting
Müstair convent, Switzerland	9th Century AD	Riederer 1997	Wall painting

Figure 1. Phases within Egyptian blue, backscatter electron image (author's photograph).

Cited works

Biek, L.
1982 'Appendix II', in N. Davey and R. Ling, *Wall Painting in Roman Britain*. London: Society for the Promotion of Roman Studies; Britannia Monograph Series No 3: 220-2.

Brill, R. H.
1999 *Chemical Analysis of Early Glasses* II. New York: The Corning Museum of Glass.

Bruni, S., F. Cariati, F. Casadio and L. Toniolo
1999 'Spectrochemical Characterization by Micro-FTIR Spectroscopy of Blue Pigments in Different Polychrome Works of Art', *Vibrational Spectroscopy* 20: 15-25.

Campbell, E.
1991 'Excavations of a wheelhouse and other Iron Age structures at Sollas, North Uist by R. J. C. Atkinson in 1957', *Proceedings of the Society of Antiquaries of Scotland* 121: 117-73.

Chase, W. T.
1968 'Egyptian Blue as a Pigment and Ceramic Material', in R. H. Brill (ed.), *Science and Archaeology*. Cambridge: MIT Press: 80-90.

Davy, H.
1815 'Some Experiments and Observations on the Colours Used in Painting by the Ancients', *Philosophical Transactions of the Royal Society, London*: 97-124.

Delamare, F.
1998 'De la composition du bleu égyptien utilisé en peinture murale gallo-romaine', in S. Colinart and M. Menu (eds), *La couleur dans la peinture et l'émaillage de l'Égypte ancienne*. Bari: Edipuglia; Centro Universitario Europeo, 177-93.

El Goresy, A. J. H., M. Abdel Razek and K. L. Weiner
1986 *Ancient Pigments in Wall Paintings of Egyptian Tombs and Temples - An Archaeometric Project*. Heidelberg: Max-Planck-Institut fur Kernphysik.

Filippakis, S. E., B. Perdikatsis and K. Assimenos
1979 'X-ray Analysis of Pigments from Vergina, Greece (Second Tomb)', *Studies in Conservation* 24: 54-8.

Filippakis, S. E., B. Perdikatsis and T. Paradellis
1976 'An Analysis of Blue Pigments from the Greek Bronze Age', *Studies in Conservation* 21: 143-53.

Hall, H. R.
1913 *Catalogue of Egyptian Scarabs, etc. in the British Museum*. London: Harris and sons.

Hillyer, L.
1984 'The Conservation of a Group of Painted Mummy Cloths from Roman Egypt', *Studies in Conservation* 29: 1-9.

Jaksch, H., W. Seipel, K. L. Weiner and A. El Goresy
1983 'Egyptian blue-Cuprorivaite a Window to Ancient Egyptian Technology', *Naturwissenschaften* 70: 525-35.

Kaczmarczyk, A. and R. E. M. Hedges
1983 *Ancient Egyptian Faience. An Analytical Survey of Egyptian Faience from Predynastic to Roman Times*. London: Aris and Phillips, Ltd.

Laurie, A. P., W. F. P. McLintock and F. D. Miles
1914 'Egyptian Blue', *Proceedings of the Royal Society*, 89A: 418-29.

Lazzarini, L.
1982 'The Discovery of Egyptian Blue in a Roman Fresco of the Mediaeval Period (Ninth Century A. D.)', *Studies in Conservation* 27: 84-6.

Lucas, A. and J. R. Harris
1962 *Ancient Egyptian Materials and Industries*, 4th edition. London: Edward Arnold Publishers Ltd.

Mirti, P., L. Appolonia, A. Casoli, R. P. Ferrari, E. Laurenti, A. Amisano Canesi and G. Chiari
1995 'Spectrochemical and Structural Studies on a Roman Sample of Egyptian Blue', *Spectrochimica Acta* 51A(3): 437-46.

Morgan, M. H.
1960 *Vitruvius: The Ten Books on Architecture*. New York: Dover Publications Inc.

Nicholson, P. T.
1995 'Glass-making and glass-working at Amarna: Some new work', *Journal of Glass Studies* 37: 11-19.

Orna, M. V., O. U. S. Orna, M. J. D. Low and N. S. Baer
1980 'Synthetic Blue Pigments: Ninth to Sixteenth Centuries. I. Literature', *Studies in Conservation* 25: 53-63.

Pabst, A.
1959 'Structures of Some Tetragonal Sheet Silicates', *Acta Crystallographica* 12: 733-9.

Perdikatsis, V.
1998 'Analysis of Greek Bronze Age Wall Painting Pigments', in S. Colinart and M. Menu (eds), *La couleur dans la peinture et l'émaillage de l'Égypte ancienne*. Bari: Edipuglia; Centro Universitario Europeo; Scienze e materiali del patrimonio culturale 4: 103-8.

Petrie, W. M. F.
1917 *Scarabs and Cylinders with Names Illustrated by the Egyptian Collection in University College, London*. London: School of Archaeology in Egypt, Constable and Co, Bernard Quaitch; British School of Archaeology in Egypt and Egyptian Research Account; Twenty first year, 1915.

Pollard, A. M. and P. R. S. Moorey
1982 'Some Analyses of Middle Assyrian Faience and Related Materials from Tell al-Rimah in Iraq', *Archaeometry* 24(1): 45-50.

Profi, S., L. Weier and S. E. Pilippakis

1974 'X-ray Analysis of Greek Bronze Age Pigments from Mycenae', *Studies in Conservation* 19: 105-12.

1976 'X-ray Analysis of Greek Bronze Age Pigments from Knossos', *Studies in Conservation* 21: 34-9.

1977 'X-ray Analysis of Greek Bronze Age Pigments from Thera (Santorini)', *Studies in Conservation* 22: 107-15.

Riederer, J.

1997 'Egyptian Blue', in E. West Fitzhugh (ed.), *Artists' Pigments* III. Washington: National Gallery of Art: 23-45.

Russell, W. J.

1892 'Egyptian Colours', in W. M. F. Petrie, *Medum*. London: David Nutt.

Sack, S. P., C. Tahk and T. Peters

1981 'A Technical Examination of an Ancient Egyptian Painting on Canvas', *Studies in Conservation* 26: 15-23.

Spurrell, F. C. J.

1895 'Notes on Egyptian Colours', *Archaeological Journal* 52: 222-39.

Stodulski, L. F., E. and R. Newman

1984 'Identification of Ancient Persian Pigments from Persepolis and Pasagadae', *Studies in Conservation* 29: 143-54.

Tite, M. S., M. Bimson and M. R. Cowell

1984 'Technological Examination of Egyptian Blue', in J. B. Lambert (ed.), *Archaeological Chemistry* III. Washington: American Chemical Society 3: 215-42.

Tite, M. S.

1987 'Characterisation of Early Vitreous materials', *Archaeometry* 29(1): 21-34.

Tite, M. S., M. Bimson and M. R. Cowell

1987 'The Technology of Egyptian Blue', in M. Bimson and I. C. Freestone (eds), *Early Vitreous Materials, British Museum*. London: The British Museum; Occasional Paper 56: 39-46.

Tite, M. S., M. Bimson and N. D. Meeks

1980 'Technological Characterisation of Egyptian Blue', *Revue D' Archaeometrie*: 296-301.

Tite, M. S.

1994 'Report on SEM Examination of Vitreous Materials from Amarna'. Oxford, Research Laboratory for Archaeology and the History of Art. Unpublished.

Ullrich, D.

1987 'Egyptian Blue and Green Frit: Characterization, History and Occurrence, Synthesis', *Pact 17*: 323-32.

THE SPECIALNESS OF SCIENCE: IT'S ALL IN THE MIND

Elizabeth Hind

Histories of science are changing. They are moving away from a philosophy that was only able to see achievements of the past in terms that present day scientists were able to recognise. Histories were used to validate and strengthen the position of science within the academic community by emphasising its supposed specialness. The definition of science is also being questioned, because it is difficult or impossible for the historian to make a judgement about whether a product of human intellectual activity is science, theology, technology or another discourse. Historians of science now recognise that they need to have an understanding of not just the science, but also the culture that produced it.

This paper will discuss the implications of this new approach to Egyptologists especially and archaeologists in general. We need to concern ourselves with not simply the products, but the processes of the science that created them; this has to be the work of a specialist on the period.

At the Current Research in Egyptology Symposium in Liverpool, 2000, I presented a paper discussing my recent revision of the translation of Moscow Mathematical Papyrus Problem 10, one of the most important problems in the extant corpus of Egyptian mathematical literature. I showed that this problem, in my opinion, could only refer to the surface area of a hemispherical object. The reaction I received after giving this paper was positive, but I had obviously failed in my role as a communicator of science. One member of the audience told me, 'I thought your paper was great, but I didn't understand a word of it!' This reaction surprised me because I had always considered the measure of how good a paper is, to be, especially in its oral form, the amount of information and understanding a member of the audience could derive from it. I therefore deduce that I was meant to understand that my presentation style was excellent, my overheads were clear and visible, my voice was loud and clear, and the speed of delivery was good, but the subject of my paper, and its content were flawed. On further investigation I discovered that many people were put off by the mathematical content of the paper; many people commented that they were 'no good' at mathematics and therefore could not understand what I was talking about. Several people approached me before I had even started my paper to tell me that they would not understand.

I have therefore decided to use this paper to explain why I think every Egyptologist should have some understanding of the mathematical and scientific culture of ancient Egypt and should face any personal reservations they may have about trying to follow the mathematical procedures. This paper will also argue that Egyptologists should be unconcerned with definitions of the modern terminology. Instead Egyptologists should try to understand the nature of the mathematical and scientific texts that were produced within the framework of the perception of the intellectual culture of ancient Egypt. Egyptologists can be forgiven if they think that there is nothing of real mathematical interest in the Rhind or the Moscow Papyri; Egyptian mathematics occupies only a tiny fraction of standard textbooks on the history of mathematics,[1] if it appears at all. A review of the commentaries on the mathematical texts of the Egyptians would leave the reader under the impression that the achievements they made were facile, barely mathematical, and arrived at by chance. The reasons for this are complicated and entrenched in the philosophy of science. A few of these ideas will be explored in order to understand the reasons for this negative standpoint on the accomplishments of the Egyptians.

Writing about mathematics and mathematicians of the past has been traditionally left to historians of science, in which mathematics has its own special subsection. These people are usually trained in science or mathematics and they take up writing its history because they are interested in the origins of the theories and formulae that they have become familiar with while studying science. Unfortunately, the history could sometimes become lost in the linear narrative of the development of these modern mathematical and scientific theories. The practitioners of the history of science are also interested in the development of their own ideas so they can question the validity of their theories by examining their origins and any underlying assumptions that were made. Mathematics is particularly prone to this linear mode of enquiry as it is considered to be pure logic. There must therefore be only one correct way, and the aim of the history of mathematics is to discover when the great advances were made and by whom. The developments are then explored so that a complete transmission of the idea from its origin to its appearance in a modern mathematical textbook can be explained. As Morris

---

[1] Cf. Boyer 1989 and Van der Waerden 1954.

Kline states 'Mathematics is also a cumulative development, that is, newer creations are built logically upon older ones, so that one must understand older results to master new ones.'[2]

This approach serves the needs of the scientific and mathematical communities and there is certainly a place for it within academic research. For Egyptologists however, this approach has little to recommend it. It is now recognised that science is just one of many human intellectual activities. Any product of the human mind is unavoidably embedded in the culture of the human that produced it. You cannot understand why it took so long for Victorian doctors to find the cause of cholera and its means of transmission, unless you understand a little bit about their morals and their ideas about the natural position and habits of the poor. Their religion and the idea of disease as the punishment of God is also an important factor if an understanding of the nature of the scientific experiments that were carried out in order to find the cause of cholera is to be obtained. It is easy to dismiss the alchemical experiments of Newton as ludicrous in a purely scientific context, but alchemy was acceptable to society at the time Newton carried them out. Histories of science are now attempting to place the scientific culture of the past within a broader cultural framework. This approach has much to recommend itself to Egyptologists. Linear accounts of the development of ideas have served the purpose of the mathematical community, but they have placed emphasis on the correctness and level of abstract thought that they contain. The concern of an Egyptologist should not be value judgements of this kind as they have little to say about the ancient Egyptian culture. Instead, a contextualised appraisal of their achievements would be more informative to an Egyptologist.

In mathematics, the way in which the culture of a mathematician may affect his work is less obvious than it is in other branches of science. This is because of the apparent pure logic at work in mathematical texts. A mathematical realist would argue that the work of a mathematician is to uncover unchanging mathematical facts, rather than inventing new mathematics. Mathematical objects are therefore completely independent of human culture. The presentation of mathematics, however, and the language used to describe it, is certainly rooted in culture. Modern mathematicians have a very aesthetic view of mathematics; almost as an art form in itself. Indeed, the work of artists such as M. C. Escher is deeply rooted in mathematical principles of tessellation and perspective. This aesthetic quality has now become desirable and it is used to evaluate mathematical texts, including ancient Egyptian texts, which are found wanting because of their deep-seated roots in applicability.[3] As Peet opines 'The outstanding feature of Egyptian mathematics is its intensely practical character'.[4]

Morris Kline is looking for this elusive beauty when he writes that compared to the Greeks 'The mathematics of the ancient Egyptians and Babylonians, is the scrawling of children just learning how to write as opposed to great literature'.[5] This statement may be true, but is practically worthless to an Egyptologist. Comparisons of this kind are not made between the religions of different cultures nor are they made between styles of architecture. No style is seen to be technically more brilliant and its aesthetic nature is seen as a point of personal taste. Why should comparisons of this type be made with mathematical achievement?[6] Children are brought up to value religious tolerance, that no one religion is better than another, but it is possible to have an absolute measure of correctness in mathematics. This has prompted comparisons of this nature that reveal more about the assumptions of modern scholars than about the society under study.

Mathematics, on one level, operates as a code or sign system; it is arbitrary and it is consensual. There is no reason why the symbols x and y for the two axes of a graph are preferred, it just makes it easier to talk about drawing graphs if simple signs are used for two of its most important features and these signs need to be consensual. Conventionally x is the horizontal axis and y is the vertical axis. There is no mathematical reason for it to be so. It would work as well if the axes were labelled with different symbols but for ease of communication an arbitrary sign system has been agreed upon. There is also no reason why algebra should be the only method for the transmission of mathematical ideas. Algebra has become the favoured method because of its neatness and the ease with which transformations and manipulations can be carried out. It should be remembered, however, that this is just shorthand for the abstract concepts that operate behind the sign system that encodes the ideas.[7]

---

[2] Kline 1962, 11.

[3] Neugebauer 1952.
[4] Peet 1923, 10.
[5] Kline 1962, 14.
[6] For further investigation into this area see Cunningham 1988.
[7] Clinton 2001 Unpublished conference paper.

Egyptologists are used to the idea that modern terms for describing human activities are not necessarily the best for describing the actions of the ancient Egyptians. Egyptologists are well aware of Hornung's argument in *Conceptions of God in Ancient Egypt*,[8] that Egyptian religion is not polytheistic nor monotheistic nor pantheistic, but something that uses some of the ideas in each of the different philosophies. The words were invented to describe modern phenomena and religions and therefore the terms cannot be expected to fit the exact circumstances of an ancient people. Egyptologists are content to use the terms, but accept important limitations. Egyptologists are also aware of the inadequacies of the English language as soon as they try to translate an Egyptian text. There is awareness of the need to be able to read texts in their original language because any text loses the nuance of its meaning as soon as it is translated into a different language. It should therefore not come as a shock to Egyptologists that the boundaries between science, mathematics, theology, magic and technology should be blurred in ancient Egypt. There should be no surprise that these words do not fully describe the activities of Egyptian scribes. The philosophy of science, which is used to determine whether a subject, document or treatise is scientific or not, has been arrived at over millennia of thought, traditionally traced back to the ancient Greeks. Applying this philosophy to modern scientific research is acceptable because scientists subscribe to it. In ancient Egypt however, they could not draw upon this resource. It is unreasonable to use the maxims of modern science to judge the origins of systematic thought. As Foucault warns:[9]

> 'Historians want to write histories of biology in the eighteenth century; but they do not realize that biology did not exist then, and the pattern of knowledge that has been familiar to us for a hundred and fifty years is not valid for a previous period. And that, if biology was unknown, there was a very simple reason for it: that life itself did not exist. All that existed was living beings, which were viewed through a grid of knowledge constituted by *natural history*.'

One Egyptologist who has attempted to integrate mathematics into a cultural examination of ancient Egypt is Barry Kemp. In his *Ancient Egypt: Anatomy of a Civilization* he includes some mathematics in the chapter entitled 'The Bureaucratic Mind', which explores administrative procedures.[10] To fully understand the content of 'account papyri' that are included as plates in the chapter, arithmetical procedure is explained with reference to examples from the Rhind Mathematical Papyrus. However, he feels that it is necessary to apologise to the reader for introducing mathematics. He writes: 'At the risk of deterring the general reader a few examples will be cited in order to convey the flavour of this kind of work [keeping accounts], which occupied a significant number of those who ran the ancient Egyptian state'.[11] The examples used by Kemp ought not to cause problems for his reader because the level of mathematics they deal with should not tax a GCSE maths student. Kemp emphasises the awkwardness felt by modern readers when faced with unit fractions. Unit fractions can be dealt with easily providing thought and care are taken and the reader has access to a calculator. They need not be the bugbear that they are supposed to be. Their unfamiliarity is only a barrier until a reader has had a chance to work through a couple of examples. They then become familiar and unproblematic as long as a calculator is nearby to double check solutions.

Kemp also persists with the notion that purity is everything in mathematics and that mathematics dealing solely with functionality is somehow a lesser mathematics. He writes: 'it reflects the basic Egyptian mentality that each problem is dealt with as a specific and individual case rather than as an application of general mathematical principles'.[12] This shows a lack of consideration for the work that went into preparing the Rhind, Moscow and other mathematical papyri. The 2/n table of the Rhind papyrus is a masterpiece because it gives the best solution from a long list of possible solutions.[13] Kemp also asserts that the Egyptians did not develop their intuition for numerical processes to create 'the subject of mathematics'.[14] Apart from the caveat previously discussed that current disciplinary margins should not be applied to an ancient text, this does not consider the obvious point that the Egyptians produced texts that dealt solely with mathematics. The structure, grammar, vocabulary and idioms of Egyptian mathematical texts are distinct from other texts. There are words in the texts such as *tp-r* and *dbn* whose precise meaning is unknown but particular to a mathematical context. It is criteria such as these that are used to identify different genres.

---

[8] Hornung 1982, 252.
[9] Foucault 1970, 127-8.

[10] Kemp 1991.
[11] ibid. 116.
[12] ibid. 116-17.
[13] Gillings 1982, 45-80.
[14] Kemp 1991, 117.

The method, goals and philosophy of scientific enquiry have developed over millennia to respond to the changing needs of society and academic culture.[15] It has become a complex activity that covers a broad range of different subjects. However, to understand the origins of science a more basic philosophy is needed. At its most fundamental level, scientific enquiry is the attempt to get a handle on the natural world. Science uses available evidence to explain natural phenomena and processes that are observable to humans. These observations can be the result of empirical experiments or just close observation of the natural world. Once this definition of the foundation of science is understood then layers of philosophy and intellectual assumption can be removed. It can then be recognised that science is just one output of intellectual activity amongst many. It must be realised that theology, mythology and literature may not be philosophically removed from science in a culture such as that of ancient Egypt. In modern society, distinct discourse communities can be recognised within the wider academic community. The distinctions between them have been developed over centuries until a situation was arrived at where the language used by a physicist is not inevitably that of a linguist or a historian. You only have to consider the scientist's preference for long noun phrases and the passive voice to show that this is the case. Subjects have become isolated from each other because it is no longer possible to be a master of all subjects. There is now too much diversity within the academic community for one practitioner to be conversant with all subjects. However, in ancient Egypt there was less specialisation and a blurring of the boundaries between fields of thought that are now recognised in the modern university. Singling out one area of modern discourse as the subject of a history supposes that these boundaries are somehow intrinsic to the way that human beings think and behave.

One of the greatest advances in the understanding of intellectual output from Egypt came recently with the publication of Marshall Clagett's three-volume sourcebook on ancient Egyptian science. The first volume of this book[16] deals with a wide range of literature including well-known pieces such as the 'Satire on the Trades' and the 'Book of Amduat' as well as tomb inscriptions, onomastica and hymns. The discussion of religious and social material in a book about the history of science is an important acknowledgement of their worth. Clagett transcends the debate between sciences, religion and the arts and

the juxtaposing validities of these different disciplines. Clagett recognises that these texts can be considered 'scientific' if the loosest definition of the word is used and he notes that natural philosophy and physics cannot be separated from religion in pharaonic Egypt. He likens conflicting anthropomorphic gods to contending forces of nature.[17] Clagett includes these texts because they attempt to explain and explore the human experience of the universe. The onomasticon he includes is recognisable as an attempt to classify, which is an honourable scientific pursuit. They emphasise that scribes were held in high regard and were rewarded well by the pharaoh. The durability of intellectual output over worldly goods was also recognised. A document, used by Clagett to show scribal immortality, which is part of a student's miscellany in Papyrus Beatty IV (BM 10684) pronounces: '(Yet) those who build tombs, their places are gone. What has become of them? I have heard the words of Imhotep and Hardedef, whose sayings are recited whole'.[18]

The importance of this new approach is in trying to examine whether there is something special in the study of science that is lacking in other disciplines. The divide between the arts, humanities and sciences is now ingrained in the present academic system. Some scientists will claim that their work is objective and purely based on experimental evidence which marks it apart from the arts and humanities subjects. Science is held to be different from other academic disciplines because of the methodical way it is carried out. However, if science is grounded in culture, then how can we be sure that scientists are uncovering the truth? What place does objectivity have in a model of the advancement of science that includes cultural influences?

The nature of science and its expression in culture are as important to a historian as an understanding of politics, society and religion, which have hitherto been the principal concerns of general historical research. Just as a historian of science cannot understand the science without understanding the cultural background because they may be the products of, if not the same mind, then the same mindset, so an Egyptologist should make it their job to understand the science to produce a complete picture of the culture under study. Discussions of religion, theology, iconography, language and art history are the staples of any undergraduate series of lectures in Egyptology. Sciences should not be ignored because of fear of

---

[15] For a more detailed exploration see Chalmers 1982.
[16] Clagett 1992.

[17] ibid.
[18] Clagett 1992, 220. Translation by Lichtheim 1973, 196-7.

complex subject matters but they should be tackled with a view to creating a holistic picture of the intellectual culture of ancient Egypt.

Elizabeth Hind
Science Communication Unit, Department of Physics, University of Liverpool

Cited works

Boyer, C. B. rev. Merzbach, U.
  1989 *A History of Mathematics* Second edition. New York: John Wiley and Sons.
Chalmers, A. F.
  1982 *What is this Thing Called Science?* Milton Keynes: Open University Press.
Clagett, M.
  1992 *Ancient Egyptian Science* I – *Knowledge and Order.* Philadelphia: Philadelphia University Press; Memoirs of the American Philosophical Society 184.
Clinton, M.
  2001 *Physical Worlds, Physical Words: Can Post Modernism Save Science?* Paper presented to 4th International Conference on Postmodernism at the University of Erlangen 23-25 November 2001.
Cunningham, A.
  1988 'Getting the Game Right: Some Plain Words on the Identity and Invention of Science', *Studies of the Historical Philosophy Society* 19, No 3: 365-89.
Foucault, M.
  1970 *The Order of Things: An Archaeology of the Human Sciences.* London: Tavistock Publications.
Gillings, R. J.
  1982 *Mathematics In the Time of the Pharaohs.* New York: Dover Publications.
Hornung, E.
  1982 *Conceptions of God in Ancient Egypt: the One and the Many,* trans. J. Baines. Ithaca: Cornell University Press.
Kemp, B. J.
  1991 *Ancient Egypt: Anatomy of a Civilization.* London: Routledge.
Kline, M.
  1962 *Mathematics: A Cultural Approach.* Reading: Addison-Wesley.
Lichtheim, M.
  1973 *Ancient Egyptian Literature* I: *The Old and Middle Kingdoms.* Berkeley: University of California Press.
Neugebauer, O.
  1952 *The Exact Sciences in Antiquity.* Princeton: The Princeton University Press.
Peet, T. E.
  1923 *The Rhind Mathematical Papyrus: British Museum 10057 and 10058.* Liverpool: The University Press of Liverpool Limited, Hodder and Stoughton Limited.
Van der Waerden, B. L.
  1954 *Science Awakening.* Trans. A. Dresden. Groningen: P. Noordhoff Ltd.

CROSSING THE NIGHT: THE DEPICTION OF MYTHOLOGICAL LANDSCAPES IN THE AM DUAT OF THE NEW KINGDOM ROYAL NECROPOLIS

Peter Robinson

Introduction

Of the sixty-two tombs so far discovered in the Valley of the Kings, many contain images depicting the deceased occupant in communion with the gods in an anticipated afterlife. There are others, however, that include scenes of fabulous afterlife lands that often contained areas of extreme danger. Here distances and directions appear to have been quite literally bent and folded. The scenes depict events that could potentially lead to the end of the world as the forces of chaos attempt to overcome order. Yet these scenes show routes that were travelled daily by great divinities, familiar with their dangers. In addition, these routes, whilst not totally familiar to ordinary mortals, have been recorded in great detail by a number of ancient artists who could be described as early cartographers.

One of the earliest of these metaphysical journeys through the New Kingdom afterlife is the Am Duat, which lines the walls of a number of the tombs in the royal necropolis (Figure 1). This text records the nightly journey of the sun god Re through the Netherworld, where he sheds his appearance of old age to re-emerge on the eastern horizon as a youthful bright sun. The Am Duat is a major text in a number of the tombs in the Valley, appearing in its entirety in five tombs within the royal necropolis.[1] In a further nine tombs, extracts of the text are incorporated within the general decorative scheme.[2] One of the tombs that contains the entire text of the Am Duat is that of Tuthmosis III (KV34), which lies hidden deep within a gully at the southern end of the main valley. With its description of the journey of the sun god and his entourage between sunset and sunrise, the Am Duat could arguably be described as a map of the afterlife recording the journey through the night.

A map can be more than just a representation of part of the Earth's surface. It can portray visible (and invisible) features of the world or equally fantasy-lands and products of one's imagination. A map can use symbols to conventionally depict features, whether they are physical, such as mountains, buildings or rivers, or notional concepts, such as accessibility to places, or perceived danger. Maps do not even have to be spatially to scale to be an effective tool. Cartographers have identified five features that make a map what it is:[3]

1. Correspondence with locations in geographic space - flat images of the earth's surface, that can be recognised as places, drawn at a scale which would encompass large areas within a small space
2. Graphical imagery - that *image* and *written direction* rather than simple data is important
3. Symbolic imagery - using 'conventional signs' and shading that indicate generalisation of real world locations
4. Prototype map effects - the use of scale bars or descriptions, legends or place names typical of maps all add to the overall perception of these images as 'maps'
5. Function - if the intention of the user is to use the 'image' as a 'map' then, in combination with the previous four features, it is likely to be perceived as a map

Is it possible to apply these cartographic features to the text of the Am Duat, to confirm the supposition that the text may be a map of some part of a metaphysical afterlife? The text mentions many divine spirits encountered by the solar entourage on its nightly journey, but also apparently shows a number of landscape features, such as desert roads, waterways and gateways that are visited along the route. One might suggest that the text could also draw on the ancient Egyptians' experiences of landscape beyond the environment of the Nile valley, and may include concepts and depictions of processes familiar nowadays to geographers and geologists in their studies of the world and its surface. The cartographic investigation of the Am Duat that follows can be applied to many of the examples of the genre within

---

[1] Tombs with full texts of the Am Duat: KV7: Ramesses II; KV9: Ramesses V/VI; KV17: Seti I; KV34: Tuthmosis II; KV35: Amenhotep II.

[2] Tombs with partial Am Duat texts: KV6: Ramesses IX; KV8: Merenptah; KV11: Ramesses III; KV15: Sety II; KV22: Amenhotep III; KV23: Ay; KV38: Tuthmosis I; KV47: Siptah; KV62: Tutankhamun. In addition, KV20: the tomb of Hatshepsut and Tuthmosis I, though undecorated, contained fifteen limestone slabs inscribed with scenes from the Am Duat, Reeves and Wilkinson 1996, 93.

[3] Vasiliev et al. 1990, 122.

the Valley of the Kings. By using the specific example of Tuthmosis III's tomb KV34, however, it should be possible to investigate some of the detailed locational symbolism of the text within the greater context of an individual tomb and its setting. KV34, in addition, contains one of the earliest and most complete examples of the text and therefore could have been produced by artists who may have had a greater understanding of the text's content and meaning.

Cardinality and arrangement of the hours

The burial chamber of KV34 is laid out in a north-east/south-west trending alignment, shaped according to some, in a cartouche form or laid out as an opened papyrus roll.[4] The Am Duat texts run along the walls of this burial chamber, divided into the twelve hours of the sun's journey through the night (Figure 2). Wilkinson has analysed some aspects of the orientation of this and other tombs of the New Kingdom.[5] He concluded that the Eighteenth Dynasty tombs of the royal necropolis were generally aligned north-south with their sarcophagus lying at right angles to this main tomb axis. KV34, it would appear, closely followed this pattern, although the tomb is actually laid out in a more north-east to south-west alignment.

Analysing the reliefs further, the sequence of hours goes in an almost clockwise sequence. Thus with the beginning of the reliefs on the eastern wall, the sequence of images goes first south, then looping back eastwards during the crucial fifth and sixth hours, before heading westwards then northward for the final part of the journey (Figure 3). In many cultures throughout the world, clockwise movement following the sun is an auspicious direction,[6] and it is natural for the sun god Amun-Re to follow his own clockwise path during the night. Evidence within the text suggests a symbolic cardinality – cardinal points of the compass are mentioned as locations in the West or in the East. Sunset takes place in the 'Horn of the

West',[7] possibly representing the Theban Peak, el-Gourna, which overlooks the royal necropolis. Looping into the Kingdom of Sokar, the entourage is said to go deeper into the western desert, before returning eastwards to arrive on the eastern horizon at the moment of sunrise. Using the real-world cardinality of space outside the tomb, these movements should be seen not as part of the tomb layout, but as part of a general global compass. In this case, sunset and other 'western' aspects of the journey take place in the eastern section of the tomb relief, and sunrise and other 'eastern' locations appear on the northern walls – in effect almost a 'mirror image' of reality.

This apparent reversal of space and time is further emphasised by the greeting and chattering of the solar baboons and others that crowd the banks during the first hour. Traditionally associated with the sunrise, they are in effect worshipping the arrival of the sun during a 'sunset'. The conventions of Egyptian art, with its peculiarities in the way it depicts space and location, force the observer to read the scenes in the reliefs from right to left, into the faces of the divinities. It is the reversal of time diagrammatically represented in the entire sequence, however, that is important, as the old, dying sun is reborn as a youthful, bright sun-disk, twelve hours later.[8]

Nowadays, the twelve hours that represent the night are measured as equal divisions of time. For the sun god, travelling on his solar bark, however, things are different. The distances for the first three hours are given within the text; Hour One – 120 *itrw* in length;[9] Hour Two – 309 *itrw* by 120; Hour Three – 309 *itrw* in length. These larger than life distances reflect the Egyptian belief that the sun covered 'millions and hundreds of thousands of *schoinoi*' in its daily course.[10] In this mythological landscape, no further measurements of the lengths of complete hours are given. Now that the tomb has been opened up to Egyptologists, it is possible to measure the space allotted to each of the hours on the walls of the tomb,

---

[4] Reeves and Wilkinson 1996, 26 noted the cartouche shape of KV34, and Hornung 1982, 71 suggested the burial chamber's form as a papyrus scroll. Clagett 1989, 472 suggested that the images were laid out on the walls as if the walls themselves formed a giant papyrus.

[5] Wilkinson 1994, Table 1, 81.

[6] Examples of clockwise directionality can be found in a number of cultural contexts. Examples from Europe include the layout and regulation of medieval Scandinavian field-systems, Roberts 1973, 54. The notion of sunwise movement amongst the Iron Age Celts of Britain are investigated by Parker Pearson 1999, 47-51, who gives a useful introduction to the subject and bibliography.

[7] Extracts from the text of the Am Duat here and elsewhere are taken from the translation in Piankoff 1954, 230-318. Though this translation is primarily based on the text from the tomb of Ramesses VI, Piankoff noted divergent variations from elsewhere within the Valley of the Kings, including KV34.

[8] Robins 1997, 124.

[9] The term *itrw* as a measure of length represents about the distance of 10.5 kilometres, Clagett 1989, 507, or about 7 miles. The term is usually translated by the Greek term *schoenus* (plural *schoenoi*), Faulkner 1962, 33. Perhaps the short length of Hour One might represent the period after sunset with its afterglow, considered maybe as part of daylight?

[10] Hornung 1982, 74; Meeks and Favard-Meeks 1996, 82.

but when this is done, some interesting figures result (Table 1). Approximately 15% of the burial chamber walls are taken up by gaps of various sorts, whether undecorated areas or doorways into the burial chamber or the side chambers. Equal division of the remaining 12 hours would represent just over 7% of the area per hour. The actual allotted space, however, is markedly different to this.

Hour One with 6.6% of the area is slightly longer in allocation than Hour Two (6.23%) and longer than Hour Three (4.07%). Clearly, space allotted to the depiction of individual hours upon the walls of Tuthmosis' burial chamber is independent of either metaphysical space or actual real time, and some other mechanism determines the area allotted.

Hour Five might give a clue to the logic behind allocation of space upon the walls here in Tuthmosis III's tomb, since that is the important resurrection scene, when the sun metamorphoses from old to young. This scene on the east wall of the chamber is the longest (13.09% of total area), occupying almost twice the space that would be expected if the hour scenes were divided up on purely mathematical lines. It could be argued that the allotment of space to individual hours might be related to the requirements of recording of individual hours and their varying amounts of texts. On the other hand, perhaps it may simply be that the original gangs of workmen, when building the tomb, wished to exploit the natural weaknesses and strengths of the bedrock encircling the tomb's burial chamber, using cracks, voids and solution hollows to develop the side chambers. After rendering the walls with a fine layer of plaster, the artists would then lay out the scenes using the available space. Without the destruction of these precious reliefs, however, it would be virtually impossible to confirm this with present technologies. In other tombs the sequence of Am Duat texts is either in perfect chronological order, or having individual hours dispersed throughout the tomb.[11]

The images of the hours and texts go some way to describing the route and topography of the journey. The text and images indicate the deities that are passed along the route and give some hints of an imagined landscape for each of the hours. At the moment of sunset, the bark of 'the flesh' of Re begins its nightly travels on a celestial river, passing rows of

deities standing on both banks that praise its arrival. Travelling through Hour Two, the solar bark crosses a region of fields, as indicated by gods brandishing ears of wheat, or sprouting wheat from their hair. Re grants land to these cereal gods and agricultural spirits, perhaps indicating some sort of divine settled agricultural community upon the banks of the Celestial river. These spirits are also charged with nourishing the solar entourage as it passes by.

From the fourth Hour, the solar bark begins a descent into a desert world, where it is dragged over sand and rock, passing snakes and scorpions, some benign, others evil. Doors bar the ways through this landscape of 'mysterious ways of Ro-setau' and secret passages. After a brief diversion to an oasis-like world of vegetation during Hour Six, the solar bark returns to the 'the cavern of Osiris'. Here the bark passes by sandbanks and dunes and the sun god's entourage fights with a personification of Apopis, the snake Neha-her, which, lying on its sandbank, attempts to hold up the divine procession, and hopes to benefit from the chaos that would result from a stopping of time.

Returning to a riverine environment during Hours Nine and Ten, the solar bark heads eastwards, to prepare for the coming sunrise. As Dawn is approached, the entourage passes a valley 'of those who are head down and cannot walk', fiery pits containing evil spirits, and goddesses of the desert, before finally coming to rest on the 'Eastern' horizon at the moment of sunrise.

Depictions of landscape

Many of the locations depicted within the Am Duat are described as 'caverns' or 'chambers' in modern translations.[12] They may indicate some religious connotation going back to the early afterlife books, such as the Pyramid Texts or Coffin Texts, and perhaps indicated the concept of an 'underworld' of subterranean passageways or related to an underworld kingdom of Osiris. In the New Kingdom, however, early royal tombs such as KV34 were hidden in clefts and gullies in the eroded limestone of the Valley of the Kings. These rock voids exploited water-eroded vertical joints and weaknesses within the otherwise fine matrix of the Theban limestones, and thus the 'caverns' of the text may well represent actual geological features, known to the tomb builders familiar with the landscape. Whilst the initial incentive

---

[11] KV35 is similar in form to KV34 and the order of hours is in chronological sequence, Porter and Moss 1973, 554. The hours in the much larger Ramesside tombs such as KV17 do not follow such an ordered and continuous sequence, ibid. 536-44.

[12] Hornung 1982, 74. The title of the Am Duat text is translated by Piankoff 1954, 230, as 'The Writing of the Hidden Chamber'.

to cut tombs in the Valley of the Kings might have been one of finding secret locations to hide royal internments, no doubt the ease with which tombs could be commenced and worked within these gullies would have proved an important factor in the use of this environment as a necropolis for over five hundred years.

The images on the walls of KV34, like those in a number of other tombs in the Valley of the Kings, are lit by the passage of the sun god in his solar bark as he travels along the central register, as the texts point out on a number of occasions. Beyond the reach of his feeble light, the utter darkness is shown by a dark band, rising up from floor level, whilst the ceiling above is speckled with the depiction of five-pointed stars arranged in a regular pattern. Yet, his light is sufficient to awaken the beings along his path, and in the later hours, they call out to him.

On a more detailed level, water is shown by the usual zig-zag hieroglyph symbol either under the floating boats or in bodies of water, as in Hour Ten. Roads in the desert regions of the text are depicted conventionally as speckled red pathways. Stones and rocks cover these routes, shown as blue, red or white speckles and patches, a practice that went back at least to the Old Kingdom. Such 'conventional signs' were used to great effect on the papyrus maps of tombs and gold mines in the later Ramesside Period as well as general depictions of desert, found in a number of private tombs in the nearby necropolis from the time of Tuthmosis' successor, Amenhotep II.[13]

It is with the Kingdom of Sokar, however, that the depiction of landscape is perhaps most interesting. Hours Four, Five and Six, it has been suggested, were the crucial resurrection scenes as the sun god is rejuvenated in preparation for the coming dawn.[14] Leaving the water, the solar bark is dragged overland on 'mysterious ways' or 'sacred roads' and through barrier doors, down through successive registers, to spend time passing around the region described as the 'mysterious cavern' of Sokar.

The landforms of desert regions are distinctive (Figure 4). Outside of the Nile valley, Egypt is a land of desert. Geographically, sand dune deserts are rare over much of the land of the pharaohs, as the area is one of hills and mountains and wind-swept rock plains. Sand

is often rapidly blown away from flat areas within the desert by a process that geographers call deflation. Instead, rock-strewn desert floor lies between deeply eroded limestone and granite cliffs. Much of the landscape between the Kom Ombo marshes in the south and the Delta in the north consists of sedimentary limestones and shales, the Valley of the Kings and the plateaux around Saqqara and Giza being no exception. Whilst granites such as those in the Eastern Hills and south of Aswan are rapidly broken down mechanically with the extreme diurnal temperature range of these desert lands, most homogenous rocks such as those limestones around present day Luxor are more resistant to breakdown, locally creating resistant cap-rock.[15] Curtis, and Rutherford and Ryan, have shown that many of the tombs of the Valley of the Kings cut through the limestones of the Theban Formation, often cutting into the softer Esna shales below.[16] Furthermore, these limestones consist of a number of layers of rock.[17] These various layers are characterised by having heterogeneous strengths and resistances, and give the formation a distinctly banded appearance. Harder, more resistant layers tend to form vertical rock faces, whilst the intervening softer layers give more subdued and sloping surfaces. The harder cap-rock forms a flat, somewhat featureless plateau, traversed by the various ancient paths between Deir el-Medina and the Valley of the Kings. Perhaps the layers of hard and soft rock may be indicated within the tombs by the depictions of zig-zag 'mysterious ways of Ro-setau' within Hours Four and Five of the Am Duat. These may be thought of as crossing not from side to side on a flat surface, but might represent a descent down a cliff side into a desert valley or wadi complex (Figure 5a).

Elsewhere within desert environments, lack of running surface water other than intermittent or ephemeral streams means that few permanent river systems are available to remove eroded rock. Intense local storms can occasionally result in flash floods. After such storms, the surface of wadi floors is covered with a poorly sorted detritus of rock, gravels and sands, having been brought down gullies and channels and dumped where the power of the water is no longer able to carry its load of sediments. In localised drainage basins, fine sediment and evaporite deposits may accumulate to create flat land surfaces

13 The tomb of Kenamun, TT93, for example, shows hunting scenes in the desert and the depiction of stone-speckled pathways, Davies 1930, plate 47a.
14 Hornung 1999, 37.

15 Bloom 1973, 34-5.
16 Curtis 1995, 129-33; Rutherford and Ryan 1995, 134-56.
17 Curtis 1995, 130.

and temporary saline lakes.[18] In the centres of these basins, the fine sediments form sandy lenses as 'playas'. Perhaps such landforms may be indicated by the 'Island of Sand' in the centre of the Kingdom of Sokar, visited by the sun god's entourage during Hour Five (Figure 5b).

Divinities

Reference has already been made to the function of some of the divinities depicted in the text, for example the corn-spirits of Hour Two. In addition, there are a number of named divinities throughout the hours whose names and positions indicate something of their nature. Naturally, the great gods Osiris, Horus, Atum and others appear.

Isis and Nephthys appear either side of a mound over what is described in the text as a 'chest' shown in Hour Five.[19] This mound and chest may allude to the grave of Osiris, as textual references to the accompanying 'executioner gods' suggest. Wilkinson pointed out that Isis and Nephthys are goddesses of direction, though normally symbolically North and South.[20] The goddess of the West appears at the introduction of the hour, confirming that the scene depicted takes place 'in the West'. Elsewhere, there are personifications of North or South, or duplicated divinities for north and south, often crowned with the appropriate headgear, confirming that the whole land of Egypt is represented in the scenes depicted. One might also consider the numerous gods and minor deities that line the route associated with locations throughout the land of Egypt, such as Anubis and Sekhmet of Thebes.[21]

Hour One shows a view of the sunset in the west with its praising divinities and protecting cobras spitting fire as they greet the arrival of the solar bark. With names like 'The one of the City', 'Opener of the Two Lands', 'Heart of the earth' and 'She of the water' they confirm that the world as a whole becomes excited at the arrival of Re. It is also possible to see the power of the land throughout the texts, with a number of instances of 'Earthquake', as well as a number of instances of boundary spirits, and 'Those who see the limits'.

For the creators of the Am Duat, the period between sunset and sunrise was a dark forbidding world, full of strange noises and happenings. Any sensible person would have retired to sleep, safely protected behind charms and amuletic magic from the chaos of a period without the life-giving sun. If one were to awake during the night, the unholy howls of wild desert animals and sounds of nature would have confirmed to mortals the cries and calls of divine spirits both good and bad, as they witnessed the journey and re-creation of the sun god. The texts of the Am Duat include these signs of the night-time distress of the divinities. During Hour Eight, doorways are flung open and the spirits rejoice. These divine calls are, however, beyond the understanding of the ordinary person, as the texts explicitly record.

Conclusion

Does the Am Duat map any real places? It is true that there are a number of references to places and directions. By far the most references are to 'generic places', to riverbanks and oases, to caverns and regions. Nonetheless the text of the Am Duat should be seen as both an artistic representation of space and time, and as one of mankind's first steps in mapping the world around him and using conventional signs to indicate the nature of the landscape depicted. The Egyptian cartographers who drew these scenes were following in a long tradition of describing the cosmological world around them. Like in much of their art, they seem to have used the experiences they gained from their environment, the cycle of sunrise and sunset, the course of the Nile, the differences between the black land, *kmt*, and red land, *dšrt*, and even the rock formations in the hills around, to great effect.[22] The landscape of the Am Duat should be seen as a mirror image of this world, a metaphysical overlay, unknown and inaccessible to the living, yet laid upon, around and within the physical environment but known only to the divinities or solar visitors who nightly might pass through its ways.[23]

The cartographic and environmental symbolism contained within the Am Duat can be seen, therefore, to expose the ancient artists' concepts of their afterlife to modern analysis:

> '...no map is a total illusion ...it contains some elements of reality and mirrors its creator's views and background... old maps can be of immense importance to students of

---

[18] Strahler and Strahler 1973, 379-381. The caustic nature of some of the salt-enriched temporary lakes of the desert might have given rise to some of the 'Lakes of Fire'.
[19] Hornung 1999, 37.
[20] Wilkinson 1995, 76.
[21] For a complete list of the various divinities and their names that appear throughout the text, see Piankoff 1954, 227-318.

[22] Robins 1997, 14.
[23] Allen 1988, 56.

history because they can reveal the mentalities of past societies, civilisations and even individuals...'[24]

Describing the afterlife began in written form at least as early as the time of the Pyramids within the tombs of royalty. The idea of a drawn and painted journey, however, began much later, with the use of the 'Book of Two Ways', indicating, amongst other concepts, recommended and difficult paths through the hereafter.[25] Other Middle Kingdom funerary texts present an elaboration of the afterlife landscape, mapping both real places and mythological regions in close proximity and in relation to funerary ritual and rites of passage.[26] These Middle Kingdom texts, however, survive in non-royal contexts, and little remains of the afterlife texts from royal locations such as the palace site of *Itj-tawy*, present day Lisht, or the royal mortuary complexes along the Nile Valley. With the emergence of the New Kingdom, afterlife texts such as the Am Duat begin to appear in royal tombs, accompanied by their graphical interpretations.

The purpose behind the Am Duat is given in the opening words of the text:

> 'The writing of the Hidden Place... [It gives us] knowledge... of the mysterious souls, knowledge of what is in the hours, ...knowledge of the gates and path over which the Great God passes...'[27]

Although Hornung suggested that Tuthmosis I's tomb, KV38, is the oldest tomb in the royal necropolis to have included the Am Duat as part of its decorative schema,[28] Romer has implied that the Am Duat first began to be used as a text within the royal tomb during the reign of Tuthmosis III.[29] Hornung has suggested that this period was a time of onomastica and classification of the world around the Egyptians.[30] The Am Duat with its lists of divinities

and locations, like a number of the texts from royal tombs, was an attempt by the ancient scholars to organise and classify the afterlife and control it through the use of knowledge. It is at that time too, that Tuthmosis III, and his mother Hatshepsut before him, began to depict geographical lands and real places in detail. Hatshepsut incorporated her geographical record of Punt in her mortuary temple Deir el-Bahri and Tuthmosis included the representation of his 'botanical garden' at Karnak Temple. Additionally, the first graphical awareness in the New Kingdom of the world beyond Egypt's borders is introduced into the decorative schema within nobles' tombs in the Theban necropolis at this time. Such imagery includes depictions of foreigners bringing exotic goods, animals and tribute from faraway places.

Finally, if the extant examples of the Am Duat in the Valley of the Kings are to be compared, the words of Reeves and Wilkinson must be borne in mind:

> 'Despite certain underlying communalities of design, no two monuments in the Valley of the Kings are alike, and unique features of design or decoration were incorporated in the planning of each structure.'[31]

The Am Duat text is only included in its entirety in five tombs within the royal necropolis. Elsewhere, extracts from the text were used, and often this was in combination with the later texts, such as the various 'Books of Day and Night' or 'Books of Gates'.[32] It would, however, be an interesting exercise to investigate the full sequencing and usage of the Am Duat throughout the tombs of the necropolis. It might then be possible to identify the ancients' full understanding of this cartographic text through time, and to detect any shifts in tomb iconography or religious emphasis. It may be significant that the sequencing of the full text entirely within the burial chamber takes place in pre-Amarna Period tombs, but that the tombs of the Nineteenth Dynasty and later place individual hours throughout the chambers and corridors of the tomb layout. Does this perhaps represent a change in the tomb designers' attitude toward the text, its function and meaning, especially when other texts were then available?

It was suggested at the start of this paper that the text of the Am Duat could be considered as a map of a

---

[24] Barber 1993, 9.
[25] Lesko 1972, passim.
[26] Willems 1996, 366-74.
[27] Introduction of the Am Duat, translated by Clagett 1989, 491.
[28] Hornung 1982, 71.
[29] Romer 1974, 122. Romer states that 'It may be observed, therefore, that neither the contents of KV38 nor its design can demonstrate that the tomb was excavated before the reign of Tuthmosis III'. If this is the case, the incorporation of the Am Duat within the burial chamber of Tuthmosis I's tomb must be at least contemporary with the reign of Tuthmosis III, and therefore of a similar date to that of KV34, even though it may be assumed to have been completed before Tuthmosis III had finished his own tomb.
[30] Hornung 1982, 71-2.

[31] Reeves and Wilkinson 1996, 25.
[32] See Porter and Moss 1973, passim, for the various decorative schemata in the royal necropolis.

metaphysical environment traversed by the solar entourage during the hours of the night. In addition, it could be argued that the Egyptians might have depicted geographical and landscape features along the route in laying out the Am Duat upon the walls of the royal burial chamber. Clearly, the text, imagery and function of the Am Duat use such cartographic criteria as place-names, indications of landscape, scales and directions to depict what must be considered nothing short of a map of the sun god's nightly journey, and a guide for the deceased king, enclosed within the burial chamber of the tomb. With their depictions of surface topography, and landforms of the desert environment included in the tomb reliefs of the Valley of the Kings, the ancient Egyptians showed a knowledge of the desert lands beyond the Nile valley. The tomb of Tuthmosis III, hidden within a cleft in the cliffs surrounding the Valley of the Kings, reflects the secret world of chambers and caverns in the text, approached by crossing waterways, agricultural land and desert outcrops before ascending and descending pathways to the kingdom of the dead. Furthermore, whilst the art of the ancient tomb-builders shows that the Egyptians thought that demons and malevolent spirits inhabited the desert wastes, their use of the natural resources derived from geomorphologically complex regions in the deserts and hills surrounding the immediate Nile valley imply a familiarity with desert and rocky environments. With their need for stone and semi-precious materials for their buildings, statuary and jewellery, as well as the experiences they gained in cutting the tombs for royalty and commoners along the desert edge, the ancient Egyptians undoubtedly were able to recognise the potentialities and the dangers of the landscapes around them. As is typical of much of the Egyptians' art, the texts of the Am Duat may not only have represented a way of understanding and explaining the afterlife, but might also have enabled the deceased king to control the metaphysical landscape. For the ancient Egyptians with their fundamental beliefs in a divine afterlife based in reality, the Am Duat was a real journey through the dangers of the night. 'We are always mapping the invisible or the unattainable... transmuting it into everything it is not... *into the real*'.[33]

Peter Robinson

---

[33] Wood 1993, 5.

Table 1: Proportion of wall reliefs occupied by individual hours within the burial chamber of KV34.

Hour		Length	Percentage of tomb wall	Expected percentage
1	Images	1.94 m	6.66%	7.07%
	Text	0.40 m		
2	Images	1.79 m	6.23%	7.07%
	Text	0.40 m		
3	Images	1.43 m	4.07%	7.07%
4	Images	1.68 m	4.78%	7.07%
5	Images	3.80 m	13.09%	7.07%
	Text	0.80 m		
6	Images	1.06 m	3.02%	7.07%
7	Images	3.00 m	9.53%	7.07%
	Text	0.35 m		
8	Images	1.92 m	5.66%	7.07%
	Text	0.07 m		
9	Images	1.67 m	4.95%	7.07%
	Text	0.07 m		
10	Images	3.35 m	9.75%	7.07%
	Text	0.07 m		
11	Images	3.10 m	9.02%	7.07%
	Text	0.07 m		
12	Images	2.80 m	8.17%	7.07%
	Text	0.07 m		
	Total Gaps	5.31 m	15.11%	15.11%
	Total length	35.15 m		

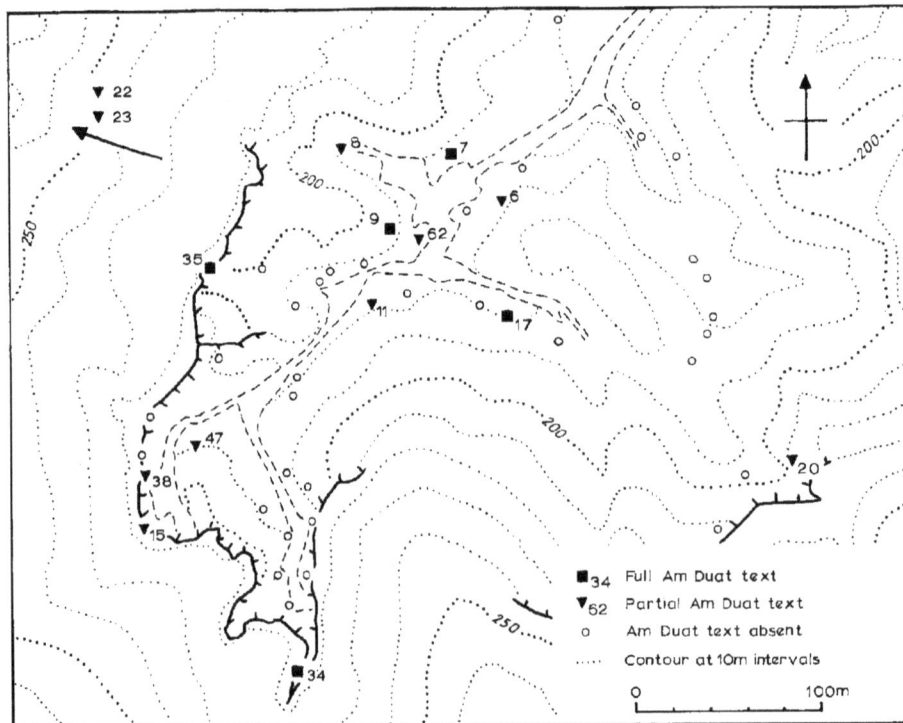

Figure 1. Locations of tombs with Am Duat texts.

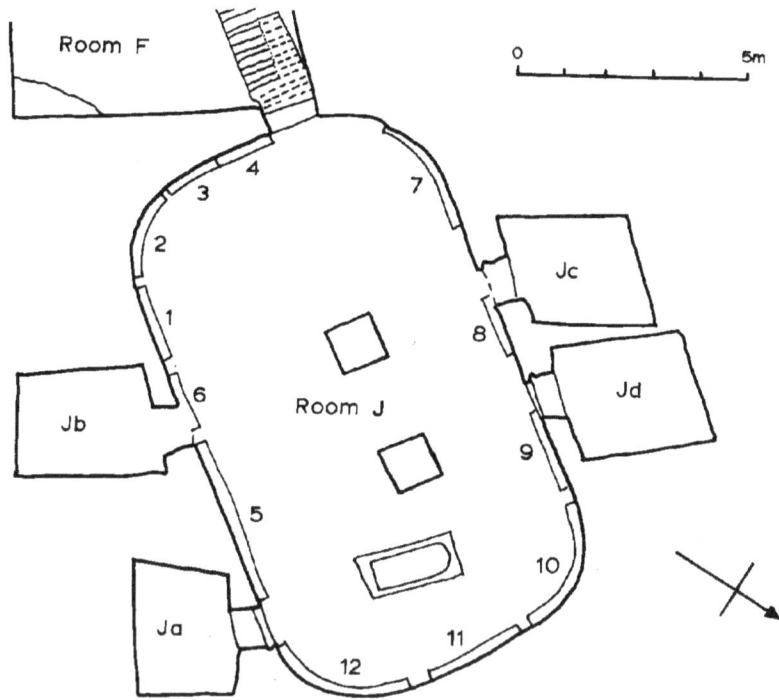

Figure 2. Sequence of hour texts within burial chamber of KV34.

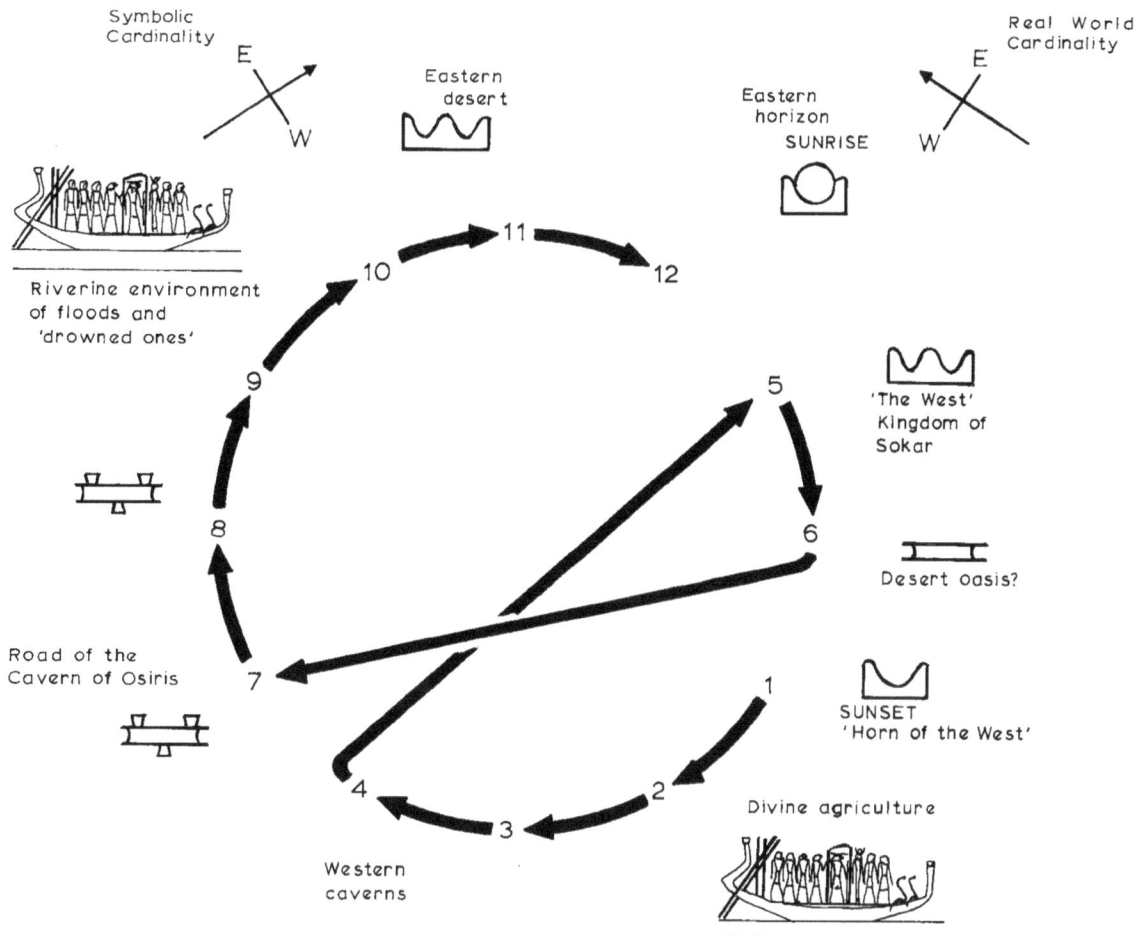

Figure 3. A symbolic journey through the night.

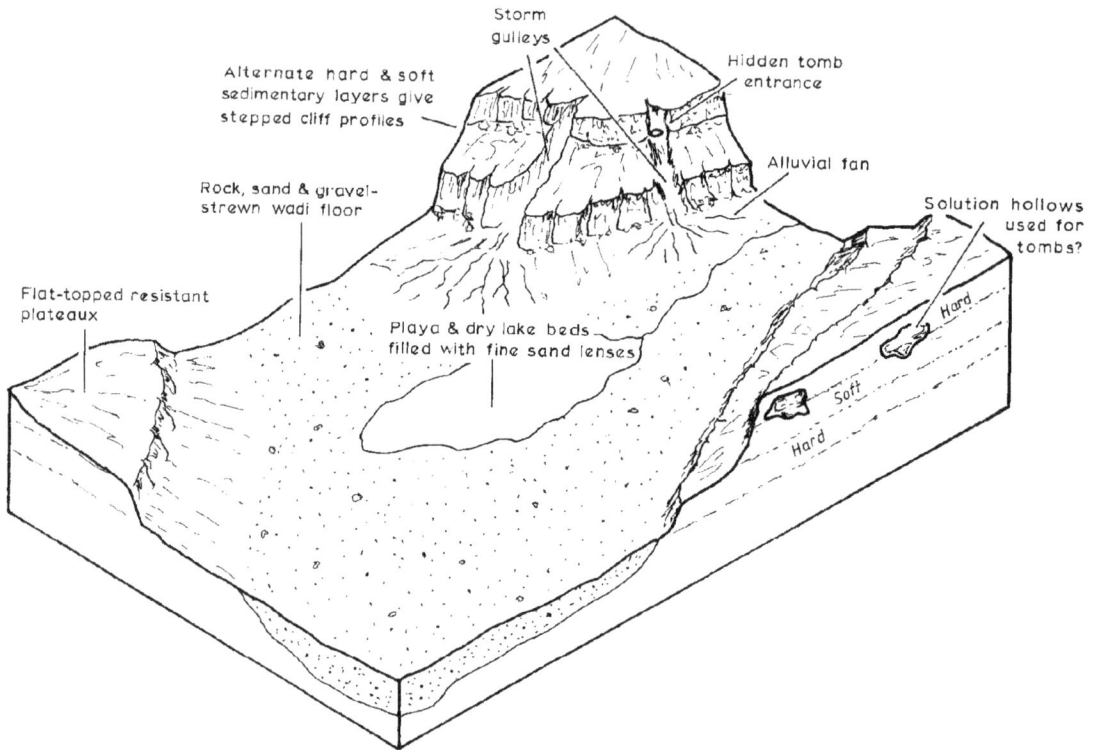

Figure 4. Desert landscape features possibly portrayed in the Am Duat.

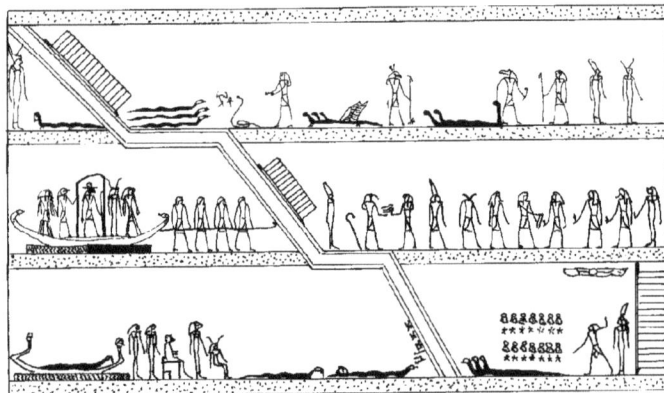

Figure 5a. The landscape of Hour Four of the Am Duat. After Piankoff 1954, Figure 77.

Figure 5b. The landscape of Hour Five of the Am Duat. After Piankoff 1954, Figure 78.

Cited works

Allen, J. P.
1988 *Genesis in Egypt: The Philosophy of Ancient Egyptian Creation Accounts.* New Haven: Yale Egyptological Seminar, Yale University; Yale Egyptological Studies 2.

Barber, P.
1993 'A Tissue of lies', in P. Barber and C. Board (eds), *Tales from the Map Room: Fact and Fiction about Maps and their Makers.* London: BBC Books, 8-9.

Bloom, A. L.
1973 *The Surface of the Earth.* London: Prentice-Hall International.

Clagett, M.
1989 *Ancient Egyptian Science: A Source Book* I. Philadelphia: American Philosophical Society.

Curtis, G. H.
1995 'Deterioration of the Royal Tombs', in R. H. Wilkinson (ed.), *Valley of the Sun Kings.* Tucson: University of Arizona Egyptian Expedition, 129-33.

Davies, N. de G.
1930 *The Tomb of Qen-amūn at Thebes* II. New York: Metropolitan Museum of Art.

Faulkner, R. O.
1962 *A Concise Dictionary of Middle Egyptian.* Oxford: Griffith Institute.

Hornung, E.
1982 *The Valley of the Kings: Horizon of Eternity.* Trans. D. Warburton. New York: Timken Press.
1999 *The Ancient Egyptian Books of the Afterlife.* Trans. D. Lorton. Ithaca: Cornell University Press.

Lesko, L. H.
1972 *The Ancient Egyptian Book of Two Ways.* Berkeley: University of California Press.

Meeks, D. and C. Favard-Meeks
1996 *Daily Life of the Egyptian Gods.* Trans. G. M. Goshgarian. London: John Murray.

Parker Pearson, M.
1999 'Food, Sex and Death: Cosmologies in the British Iron Age with Particular Reference to East Yorkshire', *Cambridge Archaeological Journal* 9:1: 43-69.

Piankoff, A.
1954 *The Tomb of Ramesses VI.* New York: Pantheon Books, Princeton University Press; Bollingen Series 40/1.

Porter, B. and R. Moss
1973 *Topographical Bibliography of Ancient Egyptian Hieroglyphic Texts, Reliefs, and Paintings* I. *The Theban Necropolis, Pt 2. Royal tombs and smaller cemeteries.* Oxford: Griffith Institute.

Reeves, N. and R. H. Wilkinson
1996 *The Complete Valley of the Kings.* London: Thames and Hudson.

Roberts, B.
1973 'Planned villages from Medieval England', in A. R. H. Baker and J. B. Harley (eds), *Man Made the Land.* Newton Abbot: David and Charles.

Robins, G.
1997 *The Art of Ancient Egypt.* London: British Museum Press.

Romer, J.
1974 'Tuthmosis I and the Bibân el-Molûk: Some Problems of Attribution', *JEA* 60: 119-33.

Rutherford, J. and D. P. Ryan
1993 'Tentative Tomb Protection Priorities, Valley of the Kings, Egypt', in R. H. Wilkinson (ed.), *Valley of the Sun Kings.* Tucson: University of Arizona Egyptian Expedition, 134-56.

Strahler, A. N. and A. H. Strahler
1973 *Environmental Geoscience: Interaction between Natural Systems and Man.* Santa Barbara, California: Hamilton.

Vasiliev, I., S. Freundschuh, D. M. Mark, G. D. Theisen and J. McAvoy
1990 'What is a map?', *The Cartographic Journal* 27: 119-23.

Willems, H.
1996 *The coffin of Heqata (Cairo JdE 36418): A Case Study of Egyptian Funerary Culture of the Early Middle Kingdom.* Leuven: Uitgeverij Peeters Departement Oriëntalistiek; Orientalia Lovaniensia Analecta 70.

Wilkinson, R. H.
1994 'Symbolic Orientation and Alignment in New Kingdom Royal Tombs and their Decoration', *JARCE* 31: 79-86.
1995 'Symbolic Orientation and Alignment in New Kingdom Royal Tombs', in R. H. Wilkinson (ed.), *Valley of the Sun Kings.* Tucson: University of Arizona Egyptian Expedition 74-81.

Wood, D.
1993 *The Power of Maps.* London: Routledge.

Trends in Burial Evidence: Evaluating Expectations for the Regional and Temporal Distribution of Mortuary Behaviour in Predynastic Egypt

Joanne M. Rowland

Introduction

The current research is focussed upon the complex issue of social transition in Egypt between the Terminal Predynastic and Early Dynastic Periods (c. 3100-2900 BC). The intention of this research is to consider societal development from the perspective of mortuary remains. In this paper I am turning from the main geographical area of concentration in my research, the Delta, in order to consider what is happening on a wider scale during this period, throughout the Nile Valley and into the Sudan. It is important to gain an understanding of the regionality and diversity of mortuary treatment in order to see how the burial practices of a specific geographical area fit into the bigger picture. This paper will firstly discuss the aims of a literature survey undertaken to examine the evidence for burial trends in the Nile Valley and the Sudan, and the ways in which the data was collated. Secondly, I will consider the archaeological evidence for differentiation and diversity in mortuary practice and, finally, review the disjuncture in mortuary behaviour both regionally and temporally, and comment upon how this can be utilised to make inferences concerning stages of societal development within communities.

Literature survey

The aims of the literature survey were threefold. Firstly, it was important to establish the degree to which the mortuary evidence expresses diversity in terms of the complexity of society within the development of the Predynastic. Secondly, to elucidate whether mortuary differentiation is apparent on an intra-cemetery scale and, furthermore, look at how this evidence can be used to enhance our understanding of the nature of the transition to state society. Thirdly, to assess how burial trends are spread geographically and temporally. This information could then be used to establish the degree to which we can see mortuary behaviour as a useful determinant in defining where socio-cultural boundaries might lie, and in what direction influence might have passed.

The data being utilised here derives from a literature survey carried out on some fifty sites in Egypt and the Sudan, dating from the Early Predynastic Period to the Early Dynastic Period. Detailed here are the types of data that were selected for the literature survey and subsequently collated within a relational database in *Access*:

- Site name and chronological period(s)
- Size, location and nature of site, extent of excavation, and evidence for looting
- Material evidence: artefact types, materials (imported/local), contexts
- Botanical/faunal evidence
- Burial evidence: quantity and types of graves, distribution and age/sex
- Differential mortuary treatment/modes of inhumation
- Details of excavators, and bibliographic references

The collection of this data is intended to contribute towards the testing of a number of hypotheses, summarised as follows:

- Social differentiation is visible within a mortuary context, and is apparent earliest in the Nile Valley
- Age and sex are determining factors in differential mortuary treatment and spatial distribution
- During the earliest phase of the Predynastic, trends of burial evidence differ most substantially between Lower Egypt and the Nile Valley
- Modes of burial show uniformity on a regional level during the Early and Middle Predynastic, and show broader geographical uniformity by the Late Predynastic/Early Dynastic
- By the Late Predynastic there is greater uniformity in the representation of social differentiation in mortuary evidence

Aspects of social differentiation

It was necessary to assess through the literature survey data when, within the Predynastic, what might be considered as social differentiation within burial sites is first apparent, how this might actually be detected from the evidence, and furthermore to ascertain what stage of societal development we might be faced with:

egalitarian, ranked, or stratified.[1] How these aspects of social development are being classified requires brief clarification. The concept of egalitarian society does not simply suggest that all members of such a society are totally equal, nor that there is no existing framework for formal ranking or stratification. Within egalitarian societies there is theoretically the opportunity for those with sufficient ability to enter positions of merit-based status.[2] Ranked societies, however, do not preserve the balance between the number of status positions and the number of people able to occupy them. In other words, there is an excess of people who are capable, or desirous, of obtaining these positions of authority.[3] The third category being considered is that of a stratified society, this being a society in which there is increasing emphasis on economic status being correlated with social status; there is also increasing differentiation in the rights of the individual or group to obtain access to basic resources, both of which create a new type of pressure within the community.[4]

Taking this into consideration, we might expect that increasing evidence for social differentiation be witnessed later in the Predynastic, together with growth in the importance of centralised/state controlled groups, as opposed to dependence on family networks. As such this privileged access to certain goods may be reflected in the burials, in terms of both the availability of certain materials and in terms of the amount of labour required for the construction of the actual grave. Certain materials and object types might reflect individual or group involvement with central organisation, which may be first witnessed at Upper Egyptian sites.

In terms of the graves, the content and variation within the grave assemblage need to be examined, as does the differentiation in types of grave architecture being employed at a site. As indicated above, both the architecture and content of graves can be revealing in terms of how typological variety suggests differential labour input and access to resources. In addition to looking at the unit of the grave itself, it is also vital to pay attention to how the graves are spatially organised, whether densely or sparsely arranged, and whether elements of zoning are apparent, for example division by age, sex, or position. Spatial organisation can thus be a useful tool when looking for divisions within hierarchy and in considering the importance placed on the age and sex of the individual within a society.

Although constraints of space do not allow for a broader discussion here, it must also be noted that there may be other indicators which could enlighten us regarding the symbolic and ideological attitudes of these communities. These include aspects of funerary rites, the evidence for which is possibly no longer preserved,[5] and variable treatment of the body, for instance those individuals who had been subjected to trauma prior to death.[6]

The evidence

The evidence for social differentiation between burials is first apparent in the Nile Valley during the Badarian Period (c. 4400-4000 BC, dates concentrated between 4400-4000 cal BC)[7] and also in the Sudan, during the Central Sudanese Neolithic tradition (calibrated averages at the site of Kadero of 4015 ± 35 BC and 4330 ± 95 BC).[8] At the site of Matmar the majority of the burials are simple oval pits, however a small number of rectangular graves were also located. Furthermore, in the early Badarian Period at Matmar cemetery 2500, an association has been established between the larger graves and females.[9] As a contrast, in the later Badarian Period cemeteries 3000/3100 there is a correlation between male burials and larger graves, with specific areas in the cemeteries set aside for male burials.[10] In terms of grave good assemblages, most commonly a single ceramic pot was placed with the deceased, although additional goods, including slate palettes and stone beads and shells, were occasionally found.[11] There is also evidence for spatial zoning and variation in grave good assemblages at burial sites associated with the Central Sudanese Neolithic Tradition. At the site of Kadero spatial zoning is apparent, with one zone containing male, female and child burials, another only male and child burials. Within these clusters there is also variation within the grave good assemblages, with the cluster containing burials of males, females and children showing very little evidence in terms of funerary provision, and a small cluster of nine graves, also of male and female adults and children, being richly provided for in terms of grave goods.[12] In Lower Egypt in what is termed the Neolithic Period, partially contemporary to the Badarian Period, while we do witness indicators of social differentiation, this is far

---

[1] Fried 1967.

[2] ibid. 28 and 33.

[3] ibid. 52.

[4] Fried 1967, 52, 186, 188-9.

[5] David 1992. Also see discussion in Rowland (in press).

[6] See discussion by Debono and Mortenson 1988, 41; Friedman 1999, 11; Maish and Friedman 1999, 6-7.

[7] Hendrickx 1999, 19; Holmes 1999, 162.

[8] Hassan 1985.

[9] Baumgartel 1974, 469.

[10] Murray 1956, 87.

[11] Holmes 1999, 162.

[12] Krzyżaniak 1984, 313.

less striking than what is apparent in the Nile Valley. At el-Omari (4600-4400 cal BC)[13] there are shallow oval burial pits, notably dug in areas that had been used for settlement, as opposed to the spatially discrete burial areas of the Nile Valley. The placement of the burials does, however, indicate zoning of burials, with most male burials located in the western area and female and child burials in the east. There is, however, very limited evidence for differentiation between burials, with grave goods being rare, with the exception of a male burial found holding a stick and a child burial found with ibex horns.[14] At Merimde Beni Salama (c. 4750-4250 cal BC),[15] however, the dead were covered in matting or animal skins and were provided with no grave goods, thus presenting no clear evidence for differentiation. Despite the above suggesting differing geographical attitudes to burial at this early stage, with clearly different levels of resource input, it is important to clarify that once burial differentiation becomes apparent in the various geographical zones, it is possible to compare levels of development occurring in the different regions, if not relative levels of input.

In Upper Egypt, differentiation becomes clearer at the site of Armant, for example, which, although containing some Badarian material culture, has burial evidence dating to Naqada IC-IIIA2 (c. 3900-3300 BC).[16] The earliest graves at Armant, those of Naqada IC and IIA date, are densely distributed small oval pits, whereas by the Naqada IIB phase a group of more sparsely distributed larger rectangular graves are present in the northern area of the site. By the Naqada IIIA Period, even larger rectangular graves are found, also sparsely distributed within two separate areas of the cemetery. In Lower Egypt during this period, the cemetery at Heliopolis shows signs of differentiation amongst the burials both in terms of the amount of grave goods provided and variability as to whether or not the bodies are wrapped.[17] It is also important to note that these burials are situated within a spatially discrete cemetery area, and no longer placed within settlement areas, as had been the case previously in the north.

Cemeteries of the Late Predynastic Period onward begin to show even clearer signs of social differentiation among the deceased. Evidence from both Kafr Tarkhan (opposite the entrance to the Fayum) and Tura (Lower Egypt) reveals much

variation in terms of the size of graves and the quantity and type of grave goods present. At Kafr Tarkhan the zoning of burials is distinct, with what are described as high status burials (distinguished by both the grave size and variety of artefacts present) of the Late Predynastic being located in specific areas in the 'valley' and 'hill' cemeteries.[18] It is also notable that there is a wider range of grave good types present, including stone and ceramic vessels, slate cosmetic palettes, beads, bracelets, and copper chisels, knives and adzes.[19] The increasing variety of types of grave good within the funerary assemblage is likewise seen at the site of el-Kadada in the Sudan, placed within the Shaheinab Neolithic phase (c. 3599-2700 BC).[20] Here the grave goods included ceramic vessels, palettes, lip-ornaments, ivory, and shells coming from the Red Sea, and differentiation is detectable in four distinct burial areas.[21]

Modes of inhumation

Having reviewed above the evidence for differentiation, primarily through variation within grave size, contents, and spatial location/zoning, it is now important to consider the range of what are here termed 'modes of inhumation' that are apparent during the Predynastic and Early Dynastic Periods. These modes have been categorised as follows: orientation of the deceased, burial position, multiple burial/secondary interments, disarticulation, evidence remaining for protection of the body, and the spatial positioning of the grave goods. Examination of these modes allows us to build up a picture of the degree to which time and geographical zones are influential factors in variability. Other reasons why differences in modes of inhumation may be discernable include kin and/or family group variations and ideological associations with descent groups.

Orientation and burial position

The most common orientation in Upper Egypt up until the Third Dynasty was for the body to be positioned with the head to the south, facing west, and in a flexed position. Castillos notes that at the Upper Egyptian site of Naqada there is 'unmatched orthodoxy' in this respect, with all of the burials in cemetery T favouring this orientation, together with the majority in cemetery B.[22] The Lower Egyptian preference from the Naqada II through III Periods

---

[13] Mortenson 1999a, 592.
[14] Midant-Reynes 2000, 122.
[15] Eiwanger 1999, 505.
[16] Hendrickx 1996, 28-43.
[17] Midant-Reynes 2000, 217.

[18] Ellis 1999, 390; Hendrickx 1996, 62.
[19] Ellis 1999, 390.
[20] Hassan 1986.
[21] Midant-Reynes 2000, 227 and 228.
[22] Castillos 1982, 34-42.

and onwards was for the body to be positioned in a flexed position with the head to the north and the face to the east. At an earlier date, however, there was a greater degree of unorthodoxy in the north than in the south. Interestingly, as noted above, by the Third Dynasty we see that the position strongly associated with Lower Egyptian burials in the Predynastic becomes the most common position throughout Egypt. The flexed attitude of the burials appears consistent geographically, through Egypt and into the Sudan, and temporally, with the main difference being the degree of flexion, which ranges from very loosely to very tightly flexed, in some instance unnaturally so, suggesting bodies having been tied into this position.[23]

Multiple / secondary burials

Cemetery sites in Upper Egypt provide evidence for multiple inhumation being practised from as early as the Badarian Period, while in the Sudan examples come from the Khartoum Neolithic Period site of el Ghaba. This practice continues through into the Early Dynastic Period, although the evidence becomes sparser after the Terminal Predynastic. There are examples of multiple burials from Hierakonpolis, Locality 6 (Naqada IIAB),[24] and within the Naqada cemeteries in Upper Egypt.[25] By contrast, however, early Lower Egyptian burial sites provide very little evidence for this practice. At el-Omari, the only example is the burial of one female together with a foetus, and there are no such burials at Merimde Beni Salama.[26] There is more evidence, however, for multiple and secondary burials during the Terminal Predynastic-Early Dynastic Periods, for example the site of Kafr Hassan Dawood in the eastern Delta.[27]

Bodily protection

It is clear that those burying the dead were concerned with providing some form of barrier between the corpse and the natural earth. There are a large number of burials where this is not the case, but it is nevertheless important to address the issue as this phenomenon occurs throughout Lower Egypt and into the Nile Valley. In so far as the methods of protection employed are concerned, a development is apparent from the early use of matting and/or animal skins, both from the Badarian burials at the site of Matmar in the Nile Valley and the sites of Merimde

Beni Salama and el-Omari in Lower Egypt, to more substantial forms of protection, i.e. coffins. Coffins develop from early examples with ceramic sides and basketry bases, at the site of el-Mahasna for example, to coffins of various shapes and sizes, made entirely from pottery.[28] In addition, there are examples of reed or basketry coffins, such as those from the site of Kafr Tarkhan, where the body was sometimes found wrapped in a mat within the coffin.[29] A further, or alternative, means of protecting the grave was through the use of roofing and lining materials such as mudbrick, mudplaster, or wood, as is the case of the wood roofing and lining found in burials at Heliopolis.[30] A further advancement in this means of protection comes from the tomb of King Den, which was originally lined with granite slabs.[31] The evidence strongly suggests an early common wish to protect the dead from the ground in which they were buried.

Spatial positioning of grave goods

Again we see a comparable development between Lower Egypt and the Nile Valley, but as suggested earlier, the Upper Egyptian burials reflect a greater input of resources to what is otherwise a common practice. Spatial positioning is best illustrated in Upper Egypt, as noted by Petrie,[32] where the more personal, or smaller objects, were placed around the body, for example daggers at the hips and knives behind the body, with larger and coarser vessels by the feet. Even at some Lower Egyptian sites, where grave goods are rare, with possibly only a single ceramic vessel, this is placed by the face, arms or legs.[33] The architectural development of additional chambers within the grave allowed for the accommodation of some of the larger vessels, previously placed by the feet. This first becomes apparent in the Nile Valley and later becomes common in the north.

Discussion of social differentiation

From the above it is possible to make a number of inferences concerning the types of societal development that are detectable in the varying regions at differing periods. From the earliest phase of Lower Egyptian evidence discussed here, the site of el-Omari indicates the possibility that there were a small number of individuals who in some way possessed greater importance/influence than other members of

[23] Midant-Reynes 2000, 227, 230.
[24] Adams 2000, 4.
[25] Petrie and Quibell 1896, 16 and 34; Midant-Reynes 2000, 188; Hoffman 1979, 114-16.
[26] Midant-Reynes 2000, 122.
[27] Hassan 2000, 38.

[28] Ayrton and Loat 1911, 5-6.
[29] Ellis 1999, 389.
[30] Ayrton and Loat 1911, 4-5.
[31] Wilkinson 1999, 236.
[32] Petrie 1920, 48.
[33] Mortenson 1999a, 593; Mortenson 1999b, 366.

the community, which may hint at the beginnings of a ranked society. The site of Merimde Beni Salama, on the other hand, provides no such distinction, and would rather suggest an egalitarian community. The Badarian culture, however, presents stronger signs of social differentiation from the mortuary evidence, suggesting very different aspects of social development, as compared with Lower Egypt, during this earliest phase. The mortuary remains from this culture indicate the possibility of a ranked society, but are not differentiated enough, nor in high enough numbers, to suggest anything beyond this stage of development. The burials of the Central Sudanese Neolithic tradition, similarly, suggest a ranked society, although the presence of a rich group of burials, including rich child burials, displays traits similar to what might be expected within a stratified society.

In Lower Egypt, the evidence coming from both Heliopolis and the cemeteries associated with the site of Maadi is suggestive of a still largely egalitarian society, with relatively low input into the grave and other funerary provisions, and little differentiation between these. Certainly the majority of child burials at Heliopolis are not provided with grave goods, suggesting achieved, rather than acquired, wealth. The cemetery at Armant in Upper Egypt, however, is indicative of what might be referred to as an emerging social elite. The site provides evidence for a development in terms of differentiation both through grave contents and through discrete spatial locations of groups of individuals.

There is increasing evidence for social differentiation as displayed through burial practice during the Late Predynastic Period onwards. At Kafr Tarkhan the range of differentiation in terms of grave size, array of grave contents, and spatial distribution suggests a change in social organisation. Also in the Sudan during the Shaheinab Neolithic, the evidence from the site of el-Kadada shows signs of more complexity in its social organisation, both in terms of distinct differentiation between the burial areas and in the increasing variation in types of grave goods being supplied.

Concluding remarks

In terms of disjuncture in burial practice the evidence reviewed here would suggest that Lower Egypt displays a greater degree of change between the Neolithic and the Early Dynastic Period. In Upper Egypt and the Sudan a more constant stream of development in social differentiation through variation within burial trends is apparent, following

through from the Badarian and Sudanese Neolithic into the Predynastic and Khartoum Neolithic. The Lower Egyptian evidence appears to reflect a change in the ideology connected with funerary ritual and this may have been driven by changes within the structural organisation of society. Furthermore, there is an increased degree of social differentiation as expressed through burial treatment. That the evidence points to an increase in cultural similarity between sites may be suggestive of increasing interaction between the activities carried out at these sites. This increase in interaction, and potentially competition, would provide an impetus for the increase in differentiation between the members of society. Changing social situations may also provide the potential for the raised importance in the role of some individuals and/or families. Therefore, when the social differentiation becomes increasingly evident within the mortuary record, the evidence reviewed above supports an inference that society is becoming increasingly non-egalitarian. Furthermore, it suggests that there is a necessity for individuals to make clear their increased status, which they may attempt to affirm in a number of ways, including through the stressing of their relationship with ancestors and through the medium of funerary ritual. To a certain degree the increased cohesion that we witness within mortuary ideology is concurrent with the increasing uniformity within and between communities. This increased uniformity may indicate that more influence is being held by Lower Egypt over Upper Egypt, in relation to the new location of the capital in the North. It may also suggest a need for Upper Egypt to encompass the traditions and ideology associated with Lower Egypt for reasons of legitimisation, and furthermore implies the necessity for an increasingly uniform ideology arising in tandem with the unified state of Egypt.

Joanne M. Rowland
Institute of Archaeology
University College London

Cited works

Adams, B.
2000 'Some Problems solved in the Locality 6 Cemetery', *Nekhen News* 12: 4-6.
Ayrton, E. R. and W. L. S. Loat
1911 *Pre-dynastic Cemetery at El-Mahasna*. London: The Egypt Exploration Fund.
Baumgartel, E. J.
1974 'Predynastic Egypt', in I. E. S. Edwards, C. J. Gadd and N. G. L. Hammond (eds), *The Cambridge*

Ancient History I, Part 1, Cambridge: Cambridge University Press, 463-97.

Castillos, J. J.
1982 *A Reappraisal of the Published Evidence on Egyptian Predynastic and Early Dynastic Cemeteries*. Toronto: Benben Publications.

David, N.
1992 'The archaeology of Ideology: Mortuary Practices in the Central Mandara Highlands, Northern Cameroon', in J. A. Sterner and N. David (eds), *An African Commitment: Papers in honour of Peter Lewis Shinnie*. Calgary: University of Calgary Press, 181-210.

Debono, F. and B. Mortenson
1988 *The Predynastic Cemetery at Heliopolis*. Mainz am Rhein: Philipp von Zabern; Deutsches Archäologisches Institut Abteilung Kairo, Archäologisches Veröffentlichungen 63.

Eiwanger, J.
1999 'Merimde Beni-Salame', in K. A. Bard (ed.), *Encyclopedia of the Archaeology of Ancient Egypt*. London: Routledge, 501-4.

Ellis, C. J.
1999 'Kafr Tarkhan (Kafr Ammar)', in K. A. Bard (ed.), *Encyclopedia of the Archaeology of Ancient Egypt*. London, Routledge, 389-90.

Fried, M. H.
1967 *The Evolution of Political Society: An Essay in Political Anthropology*. New York: Random House; Random House Studies in Anthropology 7.

Friedman, R. F.
1999 'Preliminary Report on Field Work at Hierakonpolis: 1996-1998', *JARCE* 36: 1-35.

Hassan, F. A.
1985 'Radiocarbon Chronology of Neolithic and Predynastic Sites in Upper Egypt and the Delta', *The African Archaeological Review* 3: 95-116.
1986 'Chronology of the Khartoum 'Mesolithic and Neolithic' and Related Sites in the Sudan: Statistical Analysis and Comparisons with Egypt', *African Archaeological Review* 4: 83-102.
2000 'Kafr Hassan Dawood', *EA* 16: 37-9.

Hendrickx, S.
1996 'The Relative Chronology of the Naqada Culture: Problems and Possibilities', in A. J. Spencer (ed.), *Aspects of Early Egypt*. London: British Museum Press, 36-69.
1999 'La chronologie de la préhistoire tardive et des débuts de l'histoire de l'Egypte', *Archéo-Nil* 9: 13-81.

Hoffman, M. A.
1979 *Egypt Before the Pharaohs*. New York: Knopf.

Holmes, D. L.
1999 'el-Badari District Predynastic Sites', in K. A. Bard (ed.), *Encyclopedia of the Archaeology of Ancient Egypt*. London: Routledge, 161-4.

Krzyżaniak, L.
1984 'The Neolithic Habitation at Kadero (Central Sudan)', in L. Kryżaniak and M. Kobusiewicz (eds), *Origin and Early Development of Food-producing Cultures in North-Eastern Africa*. Poznan, Polish Academy of Sciences, Poznan Branch: Poznan Archaeological Museum.

Maish, A. J. and R. F. Friedman
1999 'Pondering Paddy: Unwrapping the Mysteries of HK43', *Nekhen News* 11 (Fall 1999): 6-7.

Midant-Reynes, B.
2000 *The Prehistory of Egypt*. Oxford: Blackwell.

Mortenson, B.
1999a 'el-Omari', in K. A. Bard (ed.), *Encyclopedia of the Archaeology of Ancient Egypt*. London: Routledge, 592-4.
1999b 'Heliopolis, the Predynastic Cemetery', in K. A. Bard (ed.), *Encyclopedia of the Archaeology of Ancient Egypt*. London: Routledge, 366-7.

Murray, M. A.
1956 'Burial Customs and Beliefs in the Hereafter in Predynastic Egypt', *JEA* 42: 86-96.

Petrie, W. M. F. and J. E. Quibell
1896 *Naqada and Ballas*. London: B Quaritch.

Petrie, W. M. F.
1920 *Prehistoric Egypt*. London: B Quaritch; British School of Archaeology in Egypt and Egyptian Research Account, 23rd Year, 1917.

Rowland, J. M.
In press 'The Transition to State Society in Egypt: Problems and Possibilities of Applying Mortuary Evidence'.

Wilkinson, T. A. H.
1999 *Early Dynastic Egypt*. London: Routledge.

Nina Wahlberg

Introduction

The Hibis temple in the El-Khargeh oasis is one of the few well preserved temples from the period between the end of the New Kingdom and the beginning of the Ptolemaic Period, and one of few surviving substantial monuments from the first Persian Period in Egypt.[1] It can therefore shed interesting light on religious features of the period. This paper is specifically concerned with the depictions of the cults of Hathor and Mut in the temple and their implications for the study of the two goddesses in the period in which the reliefs were created.

The building of the Hibis temple was begun during the reign of Psammetichus II, but most of the reliefs were carved during the reign of Darius I.[2] Additional work was also carried out during the Thirtieth Dynasty, and in the Graeco-Roman Period. The temple was dedicated to Amun-Re, and its reliefs depict a large number of deities, many of whom are labelled as 'lords or ladies of Hibis', *nb(t) Hbs*, or 'who dwells in Hibis', *hry-ib(t) Hbs*. Amunet, Mut, Hathor, Isis and Nephthys are among many goddesses featured.

The sanctuary of the temple has generated much interest because its reliefs contain approximately 650 representations of deities, organised into registers.[3] The deities are depicted standing or seated, some placed on plinths, and alongside them are representations of cult symbols and priestly figures.[4] Many of the figures have lost their accompanying inscriptions, but the surviving epithets are largely geographical in nature. The deities are often called 'lady / lord of', or 'who dwells in' various places, with Thebes appearing prominently, something which is mirrored in the rest of the temple. Epithets such as *hry st wrt*, 'who is upon the great place' and *imy wi3.s/f*, 'who is in his/her bark' also feature frequently.

The commissioning of the temple reliefs and decisions about what they should include were probably the responsibility of local priests and dignitaries. This is especially important in relation to the sanctuary, as its carvings describe cults from all over the country. The choice of cults and images included must have had relevance from a local perspective, though the iconography surely also made sense in the eyes of the people in the individual geographic locations described, otherwise the geographical epithets would presumably only have had very minor importance. The emphasis on Theban and Upper Egyptian cults was most likely due to that area being the part of the Nile valley with which the oasis had closest contacts. The list appears to include the cults, throughout the country, that were most important in the eyes of the oasis people, and, through iconography, to illustrate the most salient features of those cults. The sanctuary was the most sacred location in the temple and the images probably represent the most holy and restricted aspects of the cults of the deities included.

It is possible that the list, or part of it, was designed before the Persian Period, as a similar style of decoration was also used on some Saite naoi,[5] but it seems unlikely that things that were no longer relevant would have been included. It is possible that aesthetics to some extent determined the scheme on the walls, but in essence the temple iconography had to have religious meaning. The images related to the nature of the deities, and had to do so because an important aspect of Egyptian religious art was that each image was to a certain degree the abode and embodiment of the deity it represented. Many prominent and less well known goddesses were included in the temple reliefs, and the sanctuary especially has provided a wealth of interesting images. These representations highlight many aspects of goddess cults.

Hathor

Hathor is depicted frequently on this monument, and throughout the main temple she is generally depicted as a female wearing the Hathor crown, composed of a sun disk surrounded by cow horns and sometimes accompanied by two ostrich or falcon feathers (the crown with additional plumes will henceforth be

---

[1] The reliefs from this temple mentioned in this paper were all carved in the reign of Darius I unless otherwise stated.
[2] Pottery with the cartouche of Apries was also found in the temple: Sternberg-el Hotabi 1994, 239. It may also have been extended under Hakoris, even though no cartouches survive to make this clear: Arnold 1999, 77-9, 92, 103-5, 113-15, 134.
[3] See for example: Cruz-Uribe 1988, 192-8, Osing 1990, 763-7, Sternberg-el Hotabi 1994, 245-6, Myśliwiec 2000, 142-3.
[4] The sanctuary reliefs were comprehensively published as line drawings by Davies 1953, pls. 2-5.

[5] Sternberg-el Hotabi 1994, 245-6.

called the plumed Hathor crown).[6] The sanctuary however, provides a more varied iconography for the goddess. Its south wall shows a series of seven Hathors.[7] They are called, respectively, *nb(t) Nht*, 'lady of the Sycamore'; *nb(t) Iwnt*, 'lady of Dendera'; *nb(t) Nn-nsw*, 'lady of Herakleopolis'; *nb(t) Šdšr*, 'lady of Shedesher' (situated in the Memphite area); *nb(t) W3st*, 'lady of Thebes'; *nb(t) Tpy-iḥw*, 'lady of Atfih'; and *nb(t) Imt*, 'lady of Imet' (located at modern Nebesheh in the Delta). All of these Hathor figures are depicted as female, and five of them wear only tripartite wigs. The Theban Hathor meanwhile, wears the red crown, and the Atfih Hathor a side-lock of youth. The side-lock was generally worn by child gods, and for Hathor it may symbolise her role as the daughter of the sun god Re. These seven representations of Hathor are set apart from the other figures in the register by register divisions. This suggests that the group has independent meaning, and because of the specific number of figures included its significance is likely to be tied to the mythological concept of 'the seven Hathors'. This is a commune of birth goddess forms of Hathor, assigned to the care primarily of divine and kingly children.[8] This grouping became especially prominent in Graeco-Roman temple texts, but is also in evidence in earlier material.[9] The seven Hathors were linked to birth and the destiny of children, and they are fairly frequently given different geographical epithets, as is the case here.

The next scene in the register, clearly separated from the other Hathors by a register division, shows Hathor of the Dendera nome, wearing the plumed Hathor crown on top of a cap or short-cropped hair.[10] In front of her stands a male figure who wears a side-lock of youth and shakes a sistrum before the goddess. He is identified in the text as Ihy, son of Hathor, *sḥtp ḥmt.s*, 'who pacifies her majesty'. The sistrum was an instrument especially connected with female deities and the appeasement of their dangerous aspects.[11] This scene may therefore be a

representation of a mythological occasion in which Ihy appeased his mother through the playing of the sistrum. It could however, also represent a priest performing the role of Ihy in a ritual of appeasing Hathor. Such officials are called *iḥy*-priests in Graeco-Roman inscriptions at Dendera, and one of them is depicted on a stela inscribed with the cartouches of Sheshonk V.[12] It would seem that this particular scene in the Hibis temple sanctuary emphasises the importance of this ritual in the Dendera cult, as the goddess is specifically linked to that place in the accompanying inscription.

Another representation of Hathor from the same wall unusually depicts her as a fish on a plinth.[13] It is marked *Ḥwtḥr nbt Sni*, 'Hathor, lady of Esna', and she probably acquired that form through the prominence of the fish in that cult centre.[14] This scene provides both evidence for an unusual type of iconography for the goddess, and an indication that she was venerated at Esna, for which there is little other evidence.

On the north wall of the sanctuary is another series of seven representations of Hathor.[15] The labels of these figures are damaged, but it is still clear from the remaining signs on six of them that they represent this goddess. One of the figures is not clearly stated to be Hathor, but the iconographical similarities with the other six suggest that this figure is also a representation of her. The iconography of these Hathors is somewhat different to those on the other wall. In this series cow aspects, horns and disks are prominent. Three of them have cow heads, and one is in cow-form. Two of the cow-headed females wear plumed Hathor crowns, while the third only has horns

[6] For example in the hypostyle hall and in room F: Davies 1953, pls. 9, reg. II, 17, reg. I.

[7] ibid. pl. 4, reg. III.

[8] Helck 1977, 1033.

[9] The seven Hathors are marked as birth goddesses on Papyrus Geneva Musée d'Art et d'Histoire 15274, which has been dated to the reign of Ramses III because other texts on the papyrus mention men of Deir el Medina who are known to have lived during his reign, as argued by Massart 1957, 172-3, 176. A stela which has been dated to the New Kingdom on stylistic and linguistic grounds by von Bissing and Blok 1926, 83-90, also places them in this context.

[10] Davies 1953, pl. 4, reg. III.

[11] Roberts 1984, 14, 33-5. Musical instruments were an important part of cults and helped to placate the gods and thus maintain

cosmic order: Naguib 1990, 60-2. The sistrum was for example an important part of the rite of *sḥtp Sḥmt*, 'pacifying Sekhmet', which was vital in the New Year festival: Hoenes 1976, 226, and Germond 1981, 242-53, who discussed this festival in greater detail. The most extensive descriptions of this festival and the specific rite are known from Graeco-Roman temple texts, for example in the Edfu temple.

[12] Cauville 1992, 195-202, listed a number of occurrences of this title in the Dendera temple and pointed out their function as specific appeasers of the goddess. Stela UCL 14534: the lunette of the stela shows a man, in the form of Ihy, naked and with side lock of youth, shaking a sistrum and holding a *mnit* before Hathor: Peet 1920, 56, pl. VII; Stewart 1983, 4-5, pl. 5. The man also holds the office of *ḥry sšt3 pr Ḥwtḥr*, 'master of secrets of the temple of Hathor', at Atfih.

[13] Davies 1953, pl. 4, reg. I.

[14] Gamer-Wallert 1970, 88-2, pointed out that the depiction showed a different type of fish to the one usually associated with Esna through the Graeco-Roman cult of Neith, but also that the type of fish attached to the nome in Edfu, and other, geographical lists was not always the same.

[15] Davies 1953, pl. 3, reg. VII.

on her head, as does the image of her as a cow. One of the fully female figures wears the Hathor crown, while a second wears it in combination with plumes. The final female representation wears a crown combining the sun disk with curly ram horns and the erect curls associated with Bat and Hathor. The disk and plumes connect her with the sun and sky, while the cow represents motherly love, wealth and vitality.[16]

There are cultic and mythological allusions also in these scenes. One of the standing female Hathors is flanked by two small male figures, each with one hand to his mouth and wearing a skull-cap or close cropped hair and uraeus on their brows. These probably represent Ihy and Harsomtus, both of whom were perceived as the sons of Hathor in the Graeco-Roman temple at Dendera.[17] Another one of the Hathors, seated and with a cow's head, is faced by two small male figures wearing priestly leopard skin and the side-lock of youth, one of which shakes a sistrum. These could again be representations of her sons, but are more likely to be depictions of priests officiating in her cult.[18]

It seems here too, that the images of Hathor are grouped as a unit of seven, but in this instance it is less clear, because the sequence is interrupted by an image of *Wsir ḥr Mdnt*, 'Osiris upon Medenet' (Medenet being a name for the Fayum area) and by the two child gods and two priests. This series is also not set apart by register divisions, suggesting that they form part of a greater unit, probably one formed by deities belonging to the geographical area of the Fayum and Atfih, especially as one of the cow headed females and one of the cow Hathors were labelled 'of Atfih'. It is nonetheless quite possible that their number is a direct reference to the seven Hathors, or as a more general reflection on the significance of the number seven to her cult.

The sanctuary also provides evidence of the geographical distribution of the cult of Hathor. Prominent cult centres, established long before the building of this temple, such as Dendera, Atfih, Thebes and Herakleopolis, were included, as well as a number of lesser known sites, such as Shedesher, Esna and Benu (*Bnw*), which was probably situated in

the vicinity of Diospolis Parva.[19] The list is by no means all-inclusive however, excluding for example her important centres at Gebelein and Cusae. Their exclusion suggests that from the perspective of the oasis they were less relevant.

Mut

In traditional iconography, Mut was depicted as a woman wearing the vulture-cap, a vulture covering the goddess' head with its wings trailing down her cheeks and its head rearing up on her brow, and with a double crown resting on top of the cap. This traditional iconography was also used prominently in the Hibis temple.[20] The vulture-cap was very frequently used for goddesses in the first millennium BC and marked Mut's divine female and motherly aspects, while the crown linked her to kingship and the rule of the land.[21]

The sanctuary provides a number of more unusual representations of Mut. Three of them come from a register on the west wall, which mainly contain representations of Theban deities.[22] The first of these shows her as a seated female adorned with the red crown, while the second is a lion headed female wearing the double crown. The connection between Mut and the lioness is well known, for example, through the many Sekhmet statues in her temple enclosure at Karnak,[23] but she herself was also regularly depicted with a lion head.[24] This iconographic feature marked her potential aggression and protective power. The leonine figure was given the fairly standard - in this sanctuary - epithet *Mwt ḥry st wrt ʿnḫ.ti* 'who is upon the great place, the living'. The representation of Mut wearing the red crown carries the epithet *dsr tȝwy* 'holy one of the Two Lands', which marks her as a goddess especially concerned with the rule of the country, and unusually for Mut, connects her with the Delta area. The third image depicts her as a mummiform ithyphallic figure with a lion head and tripartite wig. The ithyphallic representation of a female deity is unusual, and can be

---

16 Störk 1984, 257-63; Hermsen 1981, 64; Naguib 1990, 51-2.
17 For example in eastern crypts 1 and 2 of the Dendera temple, where both were called *sȝ Ḥwtḥr*: Chassinat 1952, 28, 43, 45, 46, 67.
18 Davies 1953, pl. 3 reg. VII. Cruz-Uribe 1988, 19, 27, suggested that they were *iwn-mwt.f*-priests, but they could also be *iḥy*-priests.

19 Davies 1953, pl. 4, reg. II; Cruz-Uribe 1988, 25. The location is likely to be Diospolis Parva, but there were also a Benu at Heliopolis and another in the Tanite nome: Gauthier 1975b, 21.
20 Examples can be found in hypostyle B, in rooms F and J and in the portico erected during the reign of Nectanebo II: Davies 1953, pls. 13, 21 reg. I, 32, 61, 63.
21 Strauss 1980, 813; Te Velde 1997, 459-60; Lesko 1999, 132, 134.
22 Davies 1953, pl. 2 reg. III.
23 See: Yoyotte 1980, 46-75.
24 Examples of leonine Mut images include an image on a bracelet from the tomb of Psusennes at Tanis: Montet 1951, 154, fig. 56 on page 152, pl. CXXI, and a bronze figurine found at Sais, Cairo CG 39128: Daressy 1906, 279, both of which were inscribed as Mut.

explained through passages in the 'Crossword hymn to Mut', a monument discovered at Karnak and containing the cartouches of Ramses VI.[25] It is a long exhortation of the glory of Mut, describing her as the protective daughter of Re, beloved of Amun and mother of Khonsu, as well as protector and ruler of the Two Lands. It also importantly said of her, 'mankind and the gods, their lives are of her giving', that she is 'she who lives by the might of her word' and 'who causes the Two Lands to live', and she was exalted '... in this her name of Creator'.[26] These statements relate to the image in the Hibis temple because they describe Mut as a creator god whose words could aid life and creation.[27] The Egyptian concept of the creation required that both male and female generative powers resided within the creator and were active in the creation. When the creator was male, which was the more widely held belief, the female power could be expressed as the hand, a feminine word in Egyptian, which the god used to masturbate, thus creating the first gods. The male aspect needed in the case of the female creator, in this case Mut, was most clearly illustrated by providing her with a phallus. The pose the figure is in, mummiform and with one hand around the erect phallus and the other holding a flail raised over her head, is usually held by fertility gods such as Amun and Min, and it may therefore also have fertility connotations. Chapter 164 of the Book of the Dead provides evidence that the Hibis sanctuary depiction was a representation of Mut and not a mistake caused by mislabelling of a figure intended as one of the aforementioned fertility gods,[28] containing as it does a vignette depicting a three-headed ithyphallic Mut and a description of the powers of the goddess.

On the north wall of the sanctuary, among deities from Memphis and Heliopolis, are another set of unusual representations of Mut.[29] In one, the goddess was called *Mwt ḥrt sn.ti*, which most likely refers to the Heliopolitan aspect of Mut known from the temple of Bastet at Bubastis, erected during the reign of Osorkon I, as *ḥrt sn.s*, 'who is under her brother'.[30] The damaged text preceding this mentions Heliopolis and the Bubastite depiction was also grouped with Heliopolitan deities, thus placing the goddess in that area. In the Hibis depiction she is a female wearing a short-cropped wig, or skullcap, and holding a shrine

with a mummiform god balanced on her head. The god is most likely Osiris, and she follows directly after Osiris lying in a shrine or tomb in the register. Mut *ḥrt sn.s*, was thus in this instance a protector of Osiris.[31]

Three images are all called Mut *ḥnty pr-Ptḥ*, 'foremost of the temple of Ptah', and are representations of her cult at Memphis.[32] The first is an enthroned figure wearing a skullcap and all-covering tight robe, iconography frequently used for Ptah himself. An interpretation of this image is therefore that it depicted Mut as adopting the primeval creative powers of Ptah in the same way as the 'Crossword hymn' suggests she did with Amun and Re. This is further emphasised by the aforementioned line in the hymn, which refers to the power of her words, as the creation of Ptah was said to come about through his words. The second image is a vulture wearing the double crown, highlighting her motherhood and her function of divine ruler of Egypt. The third depiction is a female with the skullcap, but with a wedjat eye resting on top of it. Again the 'Crossword hymn' provides an explanation, through a line naming Mut 'his (Re's) noble wedjat eye, the great one who is before him', thus marking her as the eye that protects the sun god.[33]

The final two representations of Mut on this wall appear both to be labelled by the same text: *Mwt ḥnt ꜥbwy nṯrw* 'Mut, foremost of the two horns of the gods'.[34] *ꜥbwy nṯrw* is the name of a cult centre of the goddess in the area between Memphis and Heliopolis.[35] The two images show the goddess as a female with a falcon head and white crown combined with a sun disk and uraeus and a cat on a plinth respectively. The label may refer to both figures, as the cat has no inscription of its own, even though most of the figures placed on plinths in the sanctuary had their inscriptions on the plinth. Other evidence connecting Mut with the cat, such as the decoration of

[25] Stela BM reg. no. 194, published by Stewart 1971, 87-104, pl. XXV-XXVII.
[26] Translations by Stewart 1971, 91, 93, 94, 101.
[27] This association was made by Naguib 1990, 76-7, Te Velde 1997, 458, 460, and Troy 1997, 304-5, 310.
[28] Allen 1974, 160-1; Te Velde 1997, 460.
[29] Davies 1953, pl. 3 regs. IV, V, VI.
[30] Yoyotte 1980-81, 66-70.

[31] ibid. 65-71, Yoyotte pointed out that older versions of this epithet, such as in the temple of Ramses II at Sheik Ibada, were used for representations of Mut in Heliopolitan deity groupings, and read Mut *ḥrt snwt.s*. This led him to suggest that there was a re-interpretation of the epithet sometime during the period between the reign of Ramses II and Osorkon I. From having referred to a cult of Mut 'who is under her poles', *ḥrt snwt.s*, which, as Yoyotte argued, may have referred to some form of archaic ritual edifice, it changed to signify a mythological relationship between Mut and Osiris as her brother.
[32] Davies 1953, pl. 3 reg. IV, V.
[33] Stewart 1971, 92.
[34] Davies 1953, pl. 3 reg. IV.
[35] Gauthier 1975a, 140-1, placed it somewhere between Memphis and Heliopolis, but Yoyotte 1980-81, 73-5, pinpointed the location more precisely, with the aid of, for example, its location in Papyrus Harris I's donation list.

a healing statue, strengthens the likelihood of this cat being a representation of Mut.[36] The cat icon was probably applicable to her because it was seen as a manifestation of the pacified lioness. The falcon headed image stands apart from the more frequently used iconography of Mut, and its origin is difficult to explain. As there is no room for another label it must nevertheless belong to this figure, if not to both. It is also clear from the aforementioned Memphite examples that cult centres could apply more than one facet of iconography to their deity.

The sanctuary and temple of Hibis thus give a number of cult locations also of Mut. Some of these are well known, such as Thebes, and Isheru, and Hibis, but less prominent ones, including 'the temple of Ptah' at Memphis, 'The two horns of the gods', Heliopolis, and Hermopolis were also listed.[37]

Conclusion

The representations of Hathor and Mut in the Hibis temple show that their iconography was rich and varied. It is clear that many different iconographic features were applicable within the Hibis temple itself, and the evidence from the sanctuary also suggests that this variation was applicable elsewhere. This can be seen, for example, in the three representations of Hathor labelled as belonging to Atfih, respectively in the form of a cow, a seated, cow-headed goddess with plumed Hathor crown, and a female wearing the side-lock of youth, and in the three different depictions of 'Mut, foremost in the temple of Ptah'.

Even though most of the images have geographical epithets, the iconography of the figures was not just indicative of the geographical affiliations of the goddesses. They were also suggestive of other aspects of the divinities, such as their divine characteristics and cultic functions. The Hibis temple depictions thus show Mut as the double crowned patron of the rule of Egypt, as the daughter and eye of Re, in both her aggressive leonine and pacified cat forms, as a creator goddess, and as a protector of Osiris. Hathor meanwhile, is depicted as a beautiful female, a goddess

in the solar realm, the loving mother to her sons, and as the maternal cow. Specific rituals and actions relating to her cult are also emphasised through the inclusion of her temple officials in the reliefs, and her potentially aggressive, but pacified, nature is highlighted through the depictions of the officials performing appeasement rituals.

Many of the more unusual features of iconography, all of which appear in the sanctuary, may be reflections of features of temple cult that were out of bounds for the vast majority of people, describing the most sacred aspects of the goddesses' personas. The goddesses are depicted more conventionally in the other parts of the temple, where the images were suitable for a wider audience, revealing important aspects of the deities, but possibly not the most holy ones. Votive and amuletic figurines of the goddesses too, were limited in their iconography, with Mut only depicted as a female with the vulture-cap and double crown or with a lion head, and Hathor as a female with human or cow head wearing the, sometimes plumed, Hathor crown. The iconography of the Hibis temple may thus suggest that there were varying levels of knowledge of the complexities of the cults of the goddesses, both among those who were allowed into the temple, and between them and the rest of the populace. To a certain extent, these differences were probably also a result of what people needed and wanted from their deities, with the votive images supporting the need for direct intervention in people's lives, with issues such as health and protection. Presumably the motherly, protective and country-ruling aspects of the goddesses, emphasised in the iconography of the votive and amuletic figurines, and the outer temple reliefs, were most useful to people in this context. The temples meanwhile, were concerned with the preservation of the world and the supporting and appeasing of the gods, which related more to other aspects of the divine personas.

Nina Wahlberg
The University of Birmingham

Cited works

Allen, T. G.
   1974 *The Book of the Dead or Going Forth by Day. Ideas of the Ancient Egyptians Concerning the Hereafter as Expressed in their own Terms.* Chicago: University of Chicago Press; Studies in Ancient Oriental Civilization 37.
Arnold, D.
   1999 *Temples of the Last Pharaohs.* New York, Oxford: Oxford University Press.

---

[36] Statue Cairo JE 46341, Daressy 1919, 131, 142. The statue was found at Athribis, and the biographical part of the text mentions a disruption and then restoration of the falcon temple in which the statue owner worked, which is probably a reference to the second Persian invasion, suggesting that the owner lived through that time, and the style of the statue suggests that it belongs to the Saite-Persian Period. All of this was put forward by Jelínková-Reymond 1956, xi, 68, 96-108. She did not however, mention the representations of Mut.

[37] The reference to Mut at Hermopolis is found on the south wall of the sanctuary, Davies 1953, pl. 4 reg. V; Cruz-Uribe 1988, 33.

von Bissing F. W. and H. P. Blok
1926 'Eine Weihung an die sieben Hathoren', *ZÄS* 61: 83-93.

Cauville, S.
1992 'Les prêtres «spécifiques» de Dendera', *RdE* 43: 195-202.

Chassinat, É.
1952 *Le temple de Dendara* V, *Texte*. Cairo: Institut français d'archéologie orientale.

Cruz-Uribe, E.
1988 *The Hibis Temple Project* I, *Translations, Commentary, Discussions and Sign List*. San Antonio: Van Siclen Books.

Daressy, G.
1906 *Statues de divinités. Catalogue général des antiquités égyptiennes du musée du Caire Nᵒˢ 38001-39384*. Cairo: Institut français d'archéologie orientale.
1919 'Statue de Zedher le sauveur', *ASAE* 18: 46-53.

Davies, N. de G.
1953 *The Hibis Temple in the el-Khargeh Oasis* III, *The Decoration*. New York: Metropolitan Museum of Art; Publications of the Metropolitan Museum of Art Egyptian Expedition 17.

Gamer-Wallert, I.
1970 *Fische und Fischkulte im alten Ägypten*. Wiesbaden: Otto Harrassowitz; Ägyptologische Abhandlungen 21.

Gauthier, H.
1975a *Dictionnaire des noms géographiques contenus dans les texts hiéroglyphiques* I. Osnabrück: Otto Zeller.
1975b *Dictionnaire des noms géographiques contenus dans les texts hiéroglyphiques* II. Osnabrück: Otto Zeller.

Germond, P.
1981 *Sekhmet et la protection du monde*. Geneva: Editions de Belles-Lettres; Aegyptiaca Helvetica 9.

Helck, W.
1977 'Hathoren, sieben', *LÄ* II. Wiesbaden: Otto Harrassowitz, 1033.

Hermsen, E.
1981 *Lebensbaumsymbolik im Alten Ägypten*. Köln: E. J. Brill; Arbeitsmaterialien zur Religionsgeschichte 5.

Hoenes, S-E.
1976 *Wesen und Kult der Göttin Sachmet*. Bonn: Habelt; Dissertationsdrucke, Reihe Ägyptologie 1.

Jelínková-Reymond, E.
1956 *Les inscriptions de la statue guérisseuse de Djed-Her-le-sauveur*. Cairo: Institut français d'archéologie orientale; Bibliothéque d'étude 23.

Lesko, B.
1999 *The Great Goddesses of Egypt*. Norman: University of Oklahoma Press.

Massart, A.
1957 'The Egyptian Geneva Papyrus MAH 15274', *MDAIK* 15: 172-85.

Montet, P.
1951 *La nécropole royal de Tanis* II, *Les constructions et le tombeau de Psousennès à Tanis*. Paris: Fouilles de Tanis.

Myśliwiec, K.
2000 *The Twilight of Ancient Egypt, First Millennium B. C. E.* trans. D. Lorton. Ithaca, London: Cornell University Press.

Naguib S-A.
1990 *Le clergé féminin d'Amon Thébain à la 21e dynastie*. Leuven: Peeters; Orientalia Lovaniensia Analecta 38.

Osing, J.
1990 'Zur Anlage und Dekoration des Tempels von Hibis', in S. Israelit-Groll (ed.), *Studies in Egyptology presented to Miriam Lichtheim* II. Jerusalem: Magnes Press, Hebrew University, 751-67.

Peet, T. E.
1920 'A Stela of the Reign of Sheshonk IV', *JEA* 6: 56-7.

Roberts, A.
1984 'Cult Objects of Hathor, an Iconographic Study', unpublished PhD Thesis: The University of Oxford.

Sternberg-el Hotabi, H.
1994 'Die 'Götterliste' des Sanktuars im Hibis-Tempel von El-Chargeh. Überlegungen zur Tradierung und Kodifizierung religiösen und Kulttopographischen Gedankengutes', in M. Mimas, J. Zeidler, S. Schips, S. Stöhr (eds), *Aspekte spätägyptischer Kultur. Festschrift für Erich Winter zum 65. Geburtstag*. Mainz am Rhein: Philipp Von Zabern; Aegyptiaca Treverensia, Band 7, 238-54.

Stewart, H. M.
1971 'A Crossword Hymn to Mut', *JEA* 57: 87-104.
1983 *Egyptian Stelae Reliefs and Paintings from the Petrie Collection* III, *The Late Period*. Warminster: Aris and Phillips.

Störk, L.
1984 'Rhind', in *LÄ* V. Wiesbaden: Otto Harrassowitz, 257-63.

Strauss, C.
1980 'Kronen', in *LÄ* III. Wiesbaden: Otto Harrassowitz, 811-816.

Troy, L.
1997 'Mut Enthroned', in J. van Dijk (ed.), *Essays on Ancient Egypt in Honour of Herman Te Velde*. Groningen: Styx; Egyptological Memoirs 1, 301-15.

Velde, H. Te
1997 'Mut and Other Ancient Egyptian Goddesses', in J. Phillips with L. Bell (eds), *Ancient Egypt, the Aegean, and the Near East, Studies in Honour of Martha Rhoads Bell* II. San Antonio: Van Siclen Books, 455-62.

Yoyotte, J.
1980 'Une monumentale litanie de granit. Les Sekhmet d'Aménophis III et la conjuration

permanente de la Déesse dangereuse', *BSFE* 87-88: 46-75.

1980-81 'Héra d'Héliopolis et le sacrifice humain', *École pratique des hautes études, V^e section, sciences religieuses* 89: 31-102.